FINDING
HOPE
WHEN THINGS LOOK
Hopeless

BY LARRY OLLISON
B.A., M.A., PH.D., TH.D.

1 2 3 4 5 6 7 / 30 29 28 27 26 25

Finding Hope When Things Look Hopeless
ISBN: 9781667506173

Copyright © 2017 by Dr. Larry Ollison

Published by Harrison House Publishers
www.harrisonhouse.com

"Call upon Me in the day of trouble;
I will deliver you, and you shall glorify Me."
(Psalm 50:15)

Bible hope is the intense expectation
and the confident knowledge
that what God has promised
is on its way and will come to pass.

Contents

Introduction

When it comes to hope, there are two kinds. First, there is the temporary hope that comes from the knowledge of man and earthly wisdom. Earthly hope involves the soul which requires the continual management of emotions. Spiritual problems cannot be solved by soulish methods.

The second type of hope is Bible hope. Bible hope is permanent and lasts forever. This is because Bible hope is based on the belief that God's promises have been established. Bible hope transcends the soul. It is established in the heart and because of this, emotions and surrounding circumstances are of no effect. This hope is eternal.

Biblical hope is different than wish or desire. Hope has the expectation of obtaining and the certainty of possessing. Hope knows the promise will come to pass, it just doesn't know when. Hope is ever expecting. Wish and desire can be accompanied by depression or despair because wish and desire can exist without the expectation of ever receiving. But hope is accompanied by pleasure and joy because it anticipates the good that is on its way.

Hope builds confidence, which is the highest degree of expectation, because the confidence is based on a promise from God. Hope on anything that is not solid is false hope and nothing more than a wish or a desire. True hope is grounded on substantial evidence that has been proven by God himself.

When Bible hope is established in your heart, hopelessness will become a memory. With the disappointments of life behind you, you will be able to step forward into the peace, rest, and joy that await you in the days to come, knowing that the promise of God is true. Your best days are yet to come!

> May the God of hope fill you with all joy and peace in believing, so that by the power of the Holy Spirit you may abound in hope.
>
> Romans 15:13 (ESV)

– Dr. Larry Ollison

Chapter 1

Your Dream Is Not Dead

One of the greatest hurts that can ever be experienced is living without hope. Hope is the spiritual force that keeps us moving forward. It fills each day with anticipation, excitement, and joy. With hope there is life, but when hope is stolen and our dreams are crushed, we are left with emptiness. Hopelessness brings the pain of loneliness and despair. The feeling of failure becomes almost unbearable. The Bible says hope deferred makes the heart sick (Proverbs 13:12).

However, there is hope for your life. You can break free from the heaviness and fog that is trying to pull you into darkness. Like sunshine flooding a room when the curtains are pulled back, hope will flood your soul, and you will see the possibilities that the light exposes when you discover the truth that has been hidden from you.

God has a plan for your life, and His plan is glorious. While the forces of darkness want to torment you and pull you down, the truth will illuminate the promises of God. The truth will lift you up and set you free. There is hope for you.

If you abide in My word, you are My disciples indeed. And you shall know the truth, and the truth shall make you free.

John 8:31-32

In the Hebrew language, the word for hope is *tikvah*. In Strong's Concordance (H8615) it is defined as *expectation, hope and everything that I long for*, but literally as a *cord*.[1] Hope is different than wishing and desire. Hope expects to obtain what is hoped for. *Qavah* (H6960) is the root word in Hebrew that it comes from. *Qavah means not only to expect, but to patiently wait and eagerly look for*. It also means *to collect, bind together*.[2] Patient waiting is always a part of hope.

In English, the word *hope* is more of an abstract thought, but in Hebrew the definition gives a solid visual image of a bound cord, rope, or thread. Not only can the cord be seen, but it is an object we can grasp firmly with our hands. Hebrew Bible hope is not abstract, but something that we can cling to or hold onto.

In the Bible when the two Hebrew spies entered Jericho and encountered Rahab, they swore that if she would tie a cord of scarlet thread in the window that her entire household would be spared from the impending attack. In Joshua 2:21 we are told that as the spies departed, she tied the scarlet cord in the window.

---

[1] Blue Letter Bible. "Dictionary and Word Search for *tikvah (Strong's 8615)*." Blue Letter Bible. 1996-2017. [Online]. http://www.blbclassic.org/lang/lexicon/lexicon.cfm?Strongs=H8615&t=KJV [2017 July].

[2] Blue Letter Bible. "Dictionary and Word Search for *qavah (Strong's 6960)*." Blue Letter Bible. 1996-2017. [Online]. http://www.blbclassic.org/lang/lexicon/Lexicon.cfm?Strongs=H6960&t=KJV [2017 July].

"We will be blameless of this oath of yours which you have made us swear, unless, when we come into the land, you bind this line *(tikvah)* of scarlet cord in the window through which you let us down, and unless you bring your father, your mother, your brothers, and all your father's household to your own home."

Joshua 2:17-18

In this story, the Hebrew word *tikvah* is translated as *cord (or line)* and it gives us a visual image of how hope should be viewed. Rahab placed her hope in the word of the two spies and more specifically in the scarlet thread. It was the visual covenant that she and her household would be spared when the Israelites conquered Jericho. The cord was visible, but she still had to wait for the actual manifestation of the spies' promise.

This story of Rahab reveals how Bible hope should be understood. Too often people forget that hope is rooted in waiting. While it is not often easy to wait, hope and patience by their very nature imply that waiting is necessary. For Rahab, the cord in the window represented her hope, and she trusted that she would see what she believed.[3]

I wait for the Lord, my soul waits, and in His word I do hope.

Psalm 130:5

From Hope to Fulfilled Dream

I was born in a little town in the heart of the Ozarks called Climax Springs, Missouri. It was incorporated in 1880, and by the 1950 census had reached its highest population total of 151.

---

[3] K. Gallagher, (2013). "What is Biblical Hope?" [Online]. https://graceintorah.net/2013/10/26/tikvah-hope. [2017 July].

Since that time, the population has declined! My mother's parents, Willie and Allie Park, my mother, and her eleven siblings were all born there. My father's parents, Ed and Bertha Ollison, my dad, his two brothers and sister were all born there, as well as my sister, Reta, and me. You might say I was born in a small hillbilly town comprised mainly of my relatives.

My father was a twin and my grandmother named her two sons Raymond and Ray with no middle names. Needless to say, in future years this caused many identification problems. My father was born with a bright red birthmark that covered one side of his face. In the culture of the era in which he was born, a birthmark was often considered a curse. Throughout his early life he endured many times of great hurt.

Privately, one of my uncles told me that when my dad was a young boy, he was looked down upon even by some of his own family because of his birthmark. My uncle went on to tell me that my dad continually dealt with ridicule and words of condemnation and was also told he would never amount to anything. Suffice it to say he was not given any special favors as a young man. To the contrary, favor was withheld from him in very hurtful ways.

He left the family farm in Climax Springs as a young man and fought the Nazis as a member of the 8th Air Force in England during World War II. After the war, he returned, married his childhood sweetheart, and began his quest for success.

I was five years old when my dad moved his young family from the Ozarks to Raytown, Missouri, to work at the General Motors plant in Kansas City. My father was always a hard worker and it didn't appear that he allowed insults to bother him.

While he had a full time job working at General Motors, he also was industrious. He started a small business of picking up trash barrels for people, driving them across town to the city dump, and returning their empty barrels. He did this for $2, which of course was of much greater value at that time than it is today. On the side of his pickup he had a sign that read, "Raymond Ollison and Son." On Saturdays when school was out and he wasn't working at General Motors, we ran our trash route all day long.

I remember one specific painful incident when I was thirteen years old. My dad and I had just stepped out of the truck to return an empty trash barrel when several of the neighborhood boys came over to us and started pointing at my dad's face while jeering at him. They would not quit asking, "Hey Mister, what's wrong with your face?" My dad never replied with a single word, but just continued working, ignoring the taunts. I will never forget how I felt that day. I remember crying in bed that night and thinking, "My dad didn't deserve this. He hasn't done anything wrong."

Although he had the factory job at General Motors, he had a God-given dream to move his family back to the Ozarks and live successfully. This seemed impossible, but he did not give up on his dream.

In the 1930s, the electric company built a dam on the Osage River that created a lake. This lake had 1,300 miles of shoreline and was named the Lake of the Ozarks. It was privately owned for the purpose of supplying electricity for the city of St. Louis. At the time it was built, no one could have known that it would become one of the largest and most popular boating and vacation destinations in the United States. Interestingly, this lake was near my dad's hometown of Climax Springs.

Then one day, it happened. An opportunity to move out of the city and back to the hills of the Ozarks, and to live his dream of being successful came to him, but the dream came with a price. He had been working at General Motors for fifteen years and had built up seniority, security, and amazing benefits. In order to fulfill his dream, he had to sell everything, leave his security, and venture out into the unknown. He always believed his dream was possible. He never gave up hope!

My dad was given a business opportunity to purchase a very small marina with twenty boat slips, a small repair shop with one mechanic, and a convenience store whose main product was liquor. Actually, it was the only place tourists or the locals could buy liquor for several miles.

My dad was an ordained deacon at Spring Valley Baptist Church in Raytown, Missouri. Rev. Joe C. Porter was the pastor and he and my dad were best friends. My dad was not in the ministry professionally, but he loved God with all his heart and always stood up for his Christian beliefs. He supported several mission causes and he definitely had strong convictions about alcohol!

He sold everything he owned to purchase the business. The first thing he did was take out all of the liquor, throw it away, and dedicate the business to God. All of the neighbors were shocked! I remember hearing a man named Spoke tell my father, "The liquor store was the only thing that made money. The marina was just a front!" That may have been true for the previous owner, but instead of a liquor store, there was now a hamburger and malt shop owned by a Baptist deacon. All of the neighbors thought he had lost his mind!

Every day for decades, after clocking in, the first order of the day was to gather the employees for morning prayer. That never ceased throughout my dad's life and career.

He started with nothing, but built an empire in the boating industry. With awards, trophies, and feature articles written in national magazines about his rags to riches story, my dad proved that in spite of the ridicule and taunting in his life, he did not have to accept the shame that some tried to place on him. Instead, he kept his dream alive by never losing hope. It was a difficult thing to do; nevertheless it was a choice. He chose to overcome the obstacles rather than succumbing to them. He believed deep in his heart that his dream of being successful could be attained.

Later in life, after his great success in business, he was approached by one of his friends who was a surgeon. He told my dad there was a new surgical technique available that could remove the large birthmark on his face. Interestingly, my dad chose to keep it. Money was not the issue, it was just his choice.

My dad passed away a few years ago at the age of ninety. I don't remember ever hearing him mention his birthmark, not even once. Rather than being a disgrace to him, it had become a trophy to his victory. Instead of being a burden, it became something that was insignificant.

Building the Foundation for Hope

Once while Jesus was talking with His friends, He made a powerful statement. He said that His burden was light and His yoke was easy (Matthew 11:30). In other words, He has paid the price and done all of the work for the Christian. Life should not be a struggle. If the burden we are carrying is heavy, He didn't give it to us, because His burden is light.

That does not mean there are no attacks in life. The Bible says, "Many are the afflictions of the righteous, but the Lord delivers him out of them all" (Psalm 34:19). That is good news! You may be standing in the middle of a battlefield, and a thousand may fall next to you and ten thousand may fall to your right, but if you put your trust in Him, believe His promise, and speak His promise, then nothing will by any means harm you (Psalm 91). Regardless of the size of the battle or the severity of the attack, at the end of the day you will be standing in victory if you have your trust (faith) in Him and believe His promise in your heart.

So what does that mean to us? It simply means this: God's Word says that we have been given authority over all the power of the enemy (Luke 10:19). When we speak with the authority we have been given, and truly believe in our hearts that what we say will come to pass and that we will see the victory (Mark 11:23), then worry, fear, and stress will be far from us. We can walk through the storm (battlefield) with confidence and joy.

During my years at college, I had a friend who always seemed to be at the head of the class. His grade point average was high, and he appeared to be very intelligent. For some reason, it appeared that study was easy for him. Many evenings while most of us were laboring away with the textbooks, he had completed his studies and was out on the town having fun. Years later, I discovered that although he had good grades in school, he was unable to maintain a job in his chosen profession. It seems that every time he turned in his resumè he would get the position, but after a few months on the job, he would be released.

One day while talking with one of his friends, I discovered the secret. While in college, he actually never studied, but just obtained the answers to the tests from students who had previously taken the courses. A nice way of saying this would be that he was ingenious and cut corners. The true way of saying it is this: he cheated. Although he knew the answers, when it came time to apply them, the foundation of his understanding was lacking. Having the answers became irrelevant when he couldn't explain how he got them.

Don't be like my college friend. You may have the temptation to skip the foundational truths in this chapter and look for quick-fix answers on how to obtain hope. Don't do that. That's cheating yourself! Like my college friend, if you know the answer without understanding the process to achieve the answer, in times of crisis you may fail. Let the truths found in these pages soak deep into your soul so that you understand the depth and the purpose of the promises of God. Your hope will be like the house built on the solid foundation (Matthew 7:24-25), and when the storm comes, your hope will not fail you. But you must build a solid foundation first.

In this chapter, we will explain and give scriptural detail that will build a foundation upon which you can build your hope. Our goal is for you to develop hope that will weather any storm and withstand any attack that the enemy might bring. A house built upon the sand may look good for a season (Matthew 7:26-27), but only a house built upon a strong foundation of true faith will weather the tragedies and disappointments of life.

Two Key Spiritual Truths

Before hope can be restored, there are two key spiritual truths that must be fully comprehended. Without this understanding, it will be like navigating the open seas without a compass or stars to guide you, constantly searching for direction without finding any. Without an understanding of the two key foundational truths, you will experience desperation with the temptation to just give up in the end.

Jesus once taught a parable to a large crowd who had gathered at the Sea of Galilee to hear Him. His teaching is recorded in Mark chapter 4. In this teaching, He used an illustration about a farmer who planted seed in a field. Later when He was alone with His disciples, He gave them the key to understanding the story He had told the crowd. Jesus said that the seed the man was sowing represented the Word of God. He told them it was important that they understand this parable. In fact, He went on to say if they couldn't understand this parable, all of the other parables would be meaningless to them. As a teacher, He was explaining to His students that there were things that could not be understood without first building a foundation.

The First Foundational Truth

God Cannot Lie

God is not a man, that He should lie, nor a son of man, that He should repent. Has He said, and will He not do? Or has He spoken, and will He not make it good?

Numbers 23:19

Ultimately, the key to regaining hope is anchored in the ability to believe God. Without this one key, there can never be hope. Without this one key, there can never be faith. Without this one key, there will never be true peace. Let me explain.

Relationships are built upon trust and our relationship with God is no different. When you trust someone, you could say that you have faith in them. When Jesus said in Mark 11:22, "Have faith in God," it could also be translated, "Trust God." If we fully trust Him, that means we believe what He says.

God is a good God, and He has good gifts for those who believe Him (James 1:17). The gifts are prepared and they are free. Our only requirement to receive them is to believe Him. His gifts are too numerous to list, but some of them are healing, restoration, forgiveness, eternal life, prosperity, and the healing of our broken hearts. Many of His gifts go unclaimed because of unbelief.

Not only does the Bible say that God does not lie, but also it goes on to say it is impossible (Hebrews 6:18; Titus 1:2). So as you find a promise from God, you can take it to the bank and deposit it. If you can believe it, it's yours.

The Second Foundational Truth

You Are Spirit, Soul, and Body[4]

Now may the God of peace Himself sanctify you completely; and may your whole spirit, soul, and body be preserved blameless at the coming of our Lord Jesus Christ.

1 Thessalonians 5:23

You must understand that you are a three-part being: spirit, soul, and body. You also have a spiritual heart. Every disappointment and hurt in life is harbored in the soul and manifested in the body, but the solution is in the spirit. You cannot heal the heart and create hope by only using superficial psychology. That's

---

4 For a more in-depth study of this concept, see "Spirit, Soul, and Body" (Chapter 2) in the book *The Power of Grace* by Dr. Larry Ollison (Tulsa: Harrison House Publishers, 2013) 13-36.

like putting a Band-Aid on a cancerous sore. It may cover up the problem, but it doesn't solve it.

While some of the goals of this book are to make you feel better about yourself, revitalize your dreams in life, and give you hope, the true core of this book is to drill deep into the realm of the spirit in order to anchor the Word of God in your heart so that a complete healing takes place. A complete healing is not superficial, but is grounded in the spirit. Because of this, a full grasp of who you are must be understood.

You must know that you are a three-part being—spirit, soul, and body. In the New Testament they are three distinct, different Greek words—*spirit* (*pneuma*), *soul* (*psuche*), and *body* (*soma*). One way of saying it is this: you are a spirit, you live in a body, and you possess a soul.

You were created in the likeness and image of God. God is a three-part being—Father, the Word (Jesus), and Spirit (1 John 5:7). In the same way that it is impossible to understand God without understanding that He is Father, Son, and Holy Spirit (and that these three are one), it's likewise impossible to understand who you are without knowing that you are a spirit, soul, and body.

Your spirit is the real you. When you receive Jesus Christ as your Lord and Savior, it is your spirit that is born again. At that moment, old things pass away and all things become new. When you accept Jesus as your Savior, you become a new creation. The Spirit of God moves inside your spirit to live eternally. Your death is recorded on the cross of Jesus (Romans 6:6). Your spiritual death is now in your past and no longer in your future.

Whoever lives and believes in Me shall never die.

John 11:26

Your soul is your mind, your will, your intellect, and your emotions. Your soul is where decisions are made on what you think and what you do. Your soul must decide whether to be led by the flesh or to be led by the spirit. Depending upon what your soul decides, your body will respond.

As a Christian, your body is the temple of the Holy Spirit. Not only is your own spirit contained within your body, but the Holy Spirit also lives within your spirit. Your body, while on the earth, is not eternal and it will eventually die and decay. When your body dies, your spirit must depart (James 2:26).

When you receive Jesus as your Lord and Savior, it is your spirit that is born again, not your body. Your body will be glorified in the future, but that does not happen until the Rapture of the Church.

The spirit of a Christian is born again and does not sin. However, the soul and the body are subject to their surroundings and the circumstances of life. Because the spirit of a Christian has the Holy Spirit living inside of it, we must be led by the Spirit in order to walk in truth. We could say that our deliverance and restoration come from the inside (the Spirit of God) rather than the outside (the circumstances of life).

Many scriptures that seem confusing can be clearly understood when we understand that some scriptures are talking about our spirit, some are talking about our soul, and some are talking about our body.

Because Bible hope is established in the heart, the heart must be established before Bible hope can be attained. In other words, the heart, which is the field that the Word is sown into (Mark 4:15), must be established in order for the promise contained in the seed (the Word) to grow.

The Spiritual Heart

Many times dreams are hidden in the heart and too often they die there. This does not have to be true for you. God-given dreams for your life are meant to be fulfilled, but without hope they appear as fantasy to the one holding the dream. God will not destroy the fulfillment of the dream He has placed in your heart.

The Greek word for heart is *kardia*. This word is where we get terms like cardiovascular and cardiac arrest. In other words, *kardia* simply means the organ in your chest that pumps the blood through your body.

However, in the Bible the heart is many times used metaphorically as the essence of a person. It is the unseen, non-physical place that is either good or evil. The physical heart has valves that meter the flow of life-giving substances. Likewise, the spiritual heart regulates what we say when we speak instinctively without thinking. Of course, we can take time to ponder our thoughts and make a decision on what to say. We can choose to say anything we want to say. However, when we speak instinctively without thought, those words come directly from the heart. That's what Jesus was referring to when He said, "Out of the abundance of the heart his mouth speaks" (Luke 6:45). While our calculated words can be chosen by the mind, our heart does not calculate. It simply pours out of itself what it has inside.

I have heard many great men and women of God, whom I respect and honor, teach that the heart and the spirit are the same. While this could be true in some instances, according to biblical doctrine, this cannot be a definitive truth. If the spirit and heart were the same, then a person's mouth would never instinctively utter anything evil. Why? Because the spirit is without sin

(1 John 3:9), cleansed and made righteous by the blood of Jesus (1 John 1:9), and it is possessed by the Spirit of God (Colossians 1:27), who is light and in whom there is no darkness (1 John 1:5). If the spirit and the heart were the same, then a believer would never speak anything other than faith-filled words that align with the Word of God. I have never yet met that Christian!

It is as though your heart is a field between your soul and your spirit. Good or evil seed is sown into it by the decisions made in the soul that allow words of faith from God or words of evil from the enemy through the gates of the mind. What you see and what you hear come into the realm of the soul. Thoughts taken captive and rejected are of no effect, but sights and sounds that are pondered, nurtured, and meditated upon seep into the heart and fill it. Then in times of crisis, without thought, the heart pours out through the lips what is contained in it.

I have known Christians through the years who have had good hearts, and I have also met some who have evil hearts. With both groups, their spirits had been cleansed and made righteous, but their lifestyles reflected the abundance of the Word of God or the lack of the Word of God. This is why Paul urged the church to be mature in the faith and to renew their minds with the Word. After all, the Word is the source of our hope, faith, and victory.

The soul must daily tap into the knowledge and revelation that is given by the spirit. However, it is difficult for the soul to access the wisdom of the spirit when it is drowning in the pollution of the world.

> **Those things which proceed out of the mouth come from the heart, and they defile a man.**
>
> **Matthew 15:18**

This is why the mind, which is a part of the soul, must be constantly cleansed and refreshed with the Word of God, so that the good soil between the soul and the spirit will not be polluted with bad seed or with earthly debris. Although your spirit is sealed by the Holy Spirit and darkness or corruption cannot enter it, the pollution in your heart prevents light, wisdom, understanding, guidance, and revelation (that comes from the spirit) from reaching the soul. This results in decisions that are not Spirit-led.

Setting a Course for Sound Words

Hold fast the pattern of sound words which you have heard from me, in faith and love which are in Christ Jesus.

2 Timothy 1:13

While your thoughts and your emotions are impacted by the words of others and pressures of life, your own words are a result of what you have placed in your heart. Your heart could be compared to a large ship on the ocean that turns slowly when a new course is set.

Initially your words must align with what God says about you. When He says in His Word that He will never leave you (Hebrews 13:5), when He says in His Word that He will protect you (Psalm 121:7-8), when He says in His Word that He will heal your broken heart (Luke 4:18), initially you must choose to align your words with His words.

In the beginning of this process it is usually not easy to do, because your heart has not been established. It's as though you are at the helm of a ship and you turn the small rudder (your tongue) in the direction you want to go. At first you see no change in the direction of the ship (your heart), but as you continue to keep the rudder turned in the correct direction, gradually the ship changes course. Eventually the rudder does not need to be manually changed, but only maintained because the ship (the heart) is on course and the rudder (your tongue) is naturally correct.

It's at this point the Bible tells us that faith becomes evident when, "Out of the abundance of the heart the mouth speaks" (Luke 6:45). Instead of having to think about the rudder to set the course, the rudder is following the course that is established.

Without a doubt, it's easier to maintain course than to change course. To change course means a change of belief, words, and lifestyle. To maintain course, a person must only watch for veering off the set course and when it is noticed, make the slight adjustments necessary to get back on course. The momentum of the ship helps to keep the rudder straight.

Too often people change course, but then become complacent and tend to forget, or just ignore, the job of maintaining course. This is why weight loss is such a big industry. People go on a crash diet because they discover they are overweight and off course. Because they are off course, their health and self-worth are in decay. When the pain of staying the same becomes greater than the pain of change, the crash diet begins. While on the journey to lose weight, everything is monitored even to the smallest detail. There is a goal. But all too often when the goal is obtained, and time has passed, monitoring is abandoned and slowly but steadily the ship gets off course and the weight slowly comes back.

I observed a friend who experienced this and noticed something interesting about his words. While on his diet he said things like, "I can't eat that because it isn't good for me." Then he would explain why calories, sugar, artificial additives and so on were to be avoided. However, once he obtained the proper weight, his words changed. He was not as strong in his criticism of the additives or calories, but instead verbally reasoned how it wouldn't hurt him (just this once) to eat the ice cream, the cake, etc.

Actually, he was probably right. The ice cream and cake wouldn't be a problem, "just this once," but his "just-this-once" decision opened the door for him to get off course and to gain all the weight back.

Once I heard a friend tell someone that he tried dieting to lose weight but that "diets didn't work for him." In reality, the diet did work; it's maintaining it that didn't work.

When our words change and as a result our life changes, we must maintain a pattern of good words in order to maintain our course to the fulfillment of our hopes and dreams.

The Seed and the Soil

We mentioned earlier in this chapter that Jesus taught the people through a parable (illustrated story) while at the Sea of Galilee. This parable was about a farmer who sowed seed into four different types of soil. Jesus said that some seed fell by the wayside, some fell onto stony ground, some fell among thorns, and some seed fell onto good fertile ground. The exact same seed was sown on the stony ground, by the wayside, among thorns, and also onto the good soil. There was no variation in the characteristic of the seed. However, the seed sown on the wayside, the stony ground, and among thorns did not grow properly. The only seed that produced a good harvest was the seed that fell into the good soil (Mark 4:3-8).

After He taught the people publicly, His disciples privately asked Him about the parable. Evidently the disciples didn't understand exactly what He meant when He told the story about the seed. He said to them, "To you it has been given to know the mystery of the kingdom of God; but to those who are outside, all things come in parables" (Mark 4:11), and He then explained the parable to them.

Jesus said the ones who receive the Word, but who are by the wayside, have it stolen immediately by Satan when they hear it.

Then there are others who hear the Word, but because their heart is stony, immediately they stumble. Even though they are joyful when they hear the Word, the tribulations and persecutions of life cause them to become offended so the seed never takes root and they only endure for a while.

Others have hearts that are full of thorns. When they hear the Word, the cares of the world, the deceitfulness of riches, and the desire for other things enter in and choke out the Word before it has a chance to become fruitful.

But the good news is there are those who have hearts that are fertile soil, who hunger and thirst after righteousness. When they hear the Word, they accept it, and it bears fruit—some thirty-fold, some sixty, and some a hundred. While the amount of fruit produced varies, the one constant is this: a fertile heart always receives the Word and always bears fruit (Mark 4:15-20).

How does this apply to us? The seed of hope is contained in the Word of God. The seed contains His promise of deliverance and His promise of restoration to those who will receive that seed into their heart. In order to receive the seed, you must believe in Jesus and accept Him as your Lord and Savior. As a born-again believer, you are no longer on the outside, but you are a child of the King. It has been given to you to know the mystery of the kingdom of God (Mark 4:11). Your heart is now good soil and the choice is yours on whether or not you sow the seed (the Word and His promises) into it.

As a Christian walking in faith, your heart is good soil and able to receive the promises of God to their fullest, but you must decide in the realm of your soul (your thinking and will) to do this. It's your decision whether or not you plant and your decision on how much you plant into your heart. Salvation converts your heart to a heart that is rich soil so that the seed (the Word of God) will flourish into an abundant harvest. It is the Word that grows faith.

For a Christian, the key is to sow the Word of God in your fertile heart. How do you do this? You do this by bringing the Word of God into your soul through meditating on the Word. As you meditate on the Word, you will be fertilizing the soil of your heart, which will produce a greater harvest. And what is the harvest? It is the hope you desire.

Meditating on God's Word simply requires time and repetition. Let me share this example. In the early years of my life I played the guitar, the bass, the keyboard, and sang in several musical groups. I even had the honor of playing and recording with some nationally known artists. I always enjoyed the rehearsals. In fact, I enjoyed them as much as performing on stage. The rehearsals were where I learned the melodies and chords of the new songs. It was always exciting to learn something new.

Yet, there was one distinct difference between the rehearsals and the performances. At the rehearsals we had music stands with sheet music. Actually, the sheet music was everywhere—on top of the keyboard, on the floor, and even taped to the walls! We needed our sheet music. Why? Because we were still learning the songs. But after what seemed like a few hundred times of practicing, the song was no longer just on the paper, but it was embedded in our hearts. When we stood on stage performing in front of the cheering teenagers, we could close our eyes and really get into the music because it was coming from the heart.

Interestingly, this is a God-given principle that not only works in the physical realm, but in the spiritual realm. We must practice and rehearse the Word of God what seems like hundreds of times. However, if we continually read and speak His Word, eventually it will be so deeply embedded in our hearts that it will instinctively come out of our mouths. And that's when things begin to change. Faith is the key.

So then faith comes by hearing and hearing by the Word of God.

Romans 10:17

God Has Not Forgotten

I grew up in Raytown, Missouri, and I attended Blue Ridge Elementary School. Every day I rode the school bus to and from school. All the school buses had a student who was a bus monitor. The person wore a uniform with a strap that went over his or her shoulder which connected to a belt that went around their waist. The monitor had special gloves and got to wear a badge similar to a policeman's badge.

Everyone on the bus wanted to be the bus monitor with the special seating and special honor that accompanied the position. When the bus would stop, the bus monitor, seated behind the bus driver, would stand and pull the lever that opened the school bus doors. The students would file onto the bus in the morning and off the bus in the evening with the bus monitor holding the lever. In elementary school circles, it was a big deal!

When I was in the fourth grade, I remember praying at night, "Lord, I want to be a bus monitor. Please let me be a bus monitor." Fourth and fifth grades came and went, and I didn't get to be a bus monitor. I still had hope for the sixth grade, because it was usually older students chosen by the bus driver who got the esteemed position.

The day came when they posted the list of bus monitors. It was my last chance! My name was not on the list. It was so disappointing! I remember that night asking God why He didn't answer my prayer. Even though it was a desire of my heart, it never happened. Even though I prayed, it never happened. But I finally got over it. That dream was dead. I was never going to be a bus monitor. Ever. In my life. I put the dream away.

I grew up, went to college, got married, and had children. The years went by and I became the pastor of a church. In the fall of 2001, my wife and I took a trip to Israel with Dr. Billye Brim. Although I have been to Israel many times since, this was the first time I had ever been there, and I wanted to be close to the action. I wanted to hear every word that our guide said. I didn't want to be at the back of the crowd. I wanted to hear it all!

I will never forget the first morning as we prepared to get on the bus for our first tour in Israel, Dr. Brim took me by the arm and asked me if I would be the bus monitor on bus number one. I happily agreed!

My duty each morning was to lead the people on the bus in reading Psalm 91 and, of course, I would get to sit in the special seating at the front of the bus where I could assist the tour guide as well as the bus driver while we went through our daily routine.

As I stood up on the first day to lead the reading of Psalm 91, I heard the Spirit of God speak to my heart and say, "You forgot about your dream, but I didn't!"

I was a bus monitor in Israel! That trumps Blue Ridge Elementary School! After all of those decades, even though it was a prayer I had forgotten, God had not. The prayer of a fourth grader was answered decades later in a much better way and with purpose.

So the point is this: you may think your dream is dead. I thought my dream was dead. What else could I think? It was impossible because I was no longer in school. But what seemed impossible to me was possible with God. You may have dusty, unfulfilled dreams that you have put on a shelf because you don't see how they could ever come to pass. The circumstances on the outside look like it's impossible, but the Spirit of God and the Word of God tell you this: you don't walk by sight; you walk by faith. You go by what God has spoken to you on the inside and what His Word says. Your dream is not dead; it is only sleeping.

Chapter 2

Why Are You Hopeless?

Like most people reading this book, I have encountered trials and tragedies in my life. But trials and tragedies are not the same thing. A trial is something that you can move through, and with grace and faith you can develop a powerful testimony. A financial problem or a sickness are examples of trials that many people face.

However, a tragedy is different. A tragedy can catch you off guard with great devastation. Betrayal or the sudden death of a family member that is either accidental or self-inflicted are examples of a tragedy. While going through a trial, it seems that hope for deliverance is possible, but when tragedy strikes, it feels final. Any hope of restoration seems impossible. It seems like you find yourself in a place where there is no possibility of returning to normalcy. Like a computer that has had its memory erased and its components destroyed, the only solution is to throw it away and purchase a new one. But in life, that can't be done.

When everything is destroyed by a tragedy in life, it appears like hope itself is but an unrealistic dream.

But I have good news! Whether it's a trial or a tragedy, God can restore your life so that you can walk in victory and be a testimony to the love and power of God.

Now hope does not disappoint, because the love of God has been poured out in our hearts by the Holy Spirit who was given to us.

Romans 5:5

Throughout my life I have known several family members, friends, and business associates who have taken their own lives. At the time of each tragic event, I did not notice any connection, but as the years passed I began to notice that there was a common denominator in all these tragic stories.

My grandfather was a farmer all his life. He had livestock and fields, which he harvested every year. His large family worked on the farm with him. He was well known in the community and had served in World War I in the U.S. Army. My memories of him are fond. I remember him sitting in his chair in his bib overalls playing with the younger grandchildren. He liked to tease us by sticking out his leg as we ran by him and pretend like he was going to trip us. I will never forget his hearty laugh.

When I was nine years old, my grandpa took a rifle and shot himself. I will never forget the day my mom and her brothers and sisters sat around the living room after the funeral trying to figure out why their dad had done this. At the funeral that morning, I remember my grandma going up to the casket, reaching in and grabbing my grandpa by the lapels of his burial suit and screaming, "Willie, why did you do it? Why did you do it?" Quite honestly, earlier he had a stroke, and it had deeply affected him. But at some point in time, he made a choice. The choices people make not only affect themselves, but it can affect their children and their grandchildren and even unborn generations. What motivated my grandfather to take his life?

An Attack on Our Young Ministry

One of the callings on my life is to write and publish books. In the early years of our ministry, I had no idea how to accomplish this. Although I had a book that I wanted to publish, I did not know how to go about getting it printed. Then one day, I met a man who had a printing business with the ability to publish my work. We worked together tirelessly for many months and the first edition of *God's Plan for Handling Stress* was published.

Jesus said that the enemy comes to steal, kill, and destroy. Not only does he want to do this on a personal level, but the enemy also wants to do this on a ministry level whenever possible. And like a lion seeking the weakest animal in the herd, the devil will single out individuals for destruction. He uses hopelessness as a weapon to seduce individuals to self-destruct.

This gentleman who printed my book was a good man. Our ministry was just beginning to move and make national progress in publishing books. One morning this man's wife was taking a shower when she heard a strange noise in the other room. After her shower, she put on her house robe and went out to speak to her husband and there he was. He had taken his life with a gun. I officiated his funeral in Kansas City. What motivated my business associate to take his life?

While his death was a tragedy for his family, it was also a great tragedy for our ministry. At the time of his death, we had flyers, tracks, booklets, and newsletters ready to be printed. His death closed his business and stalled the publications department of our ministry for years because he was the only printer in the area at the time.

Throughout my decades of ministry, I have ministered to dozens of families who have had a family member that committed suicide. When you look at all these tragedies, there is a common denominator that becomes evident. What motivated each of them to take such a drastic action? In each and every case the common denominator is that for a moment of time they lost all hope. Maybe they didn't lose hope for a long period of time, because it only takes a few moments of being hopeless to get to a place where you can't turn back.

His Hand Is Always There for You

When Jesus was walking on the water, He called Peter to come to Him. Peter got out of the boat and started walking on the water toward Jesus. As long as he was looking at Jesus, he walked on the water. But when Peter looked around at the severity of the storm, he began to sink. Jesus reached out, took him by the hand, and saved him (Matthew 14:25-32).

When you feel like you have reached the end of your rope, or feel like you are on the edge of a cliff about to fall, or even feel like you are drowning in hopelessness, put your eyes on Jesus. Stretch out your hand to Him, and He will rescue you (Psalm 50:15). No matter how desperate you feel, no matter how far you have sunk, no matter how hopeless it seems, His hand is always there waiting for you to reach out and take it!

For those who have taken their lives or experienced a tragedy that ended their life, they have completed their journey on earth and are now awaiting the resurrection. But for you who remain, their departure does not have to destroy your life. There is hope and there is victory for you. Do not give up. You will be set free from the bondage of guilt and pain if you do not lose heart.

That is why we never give up. Though our bodies are dying, our spirits are being renewed every day.

                              2 Corinthians 4:16 (NLT)

'You're Going to Die'

When the devil attacks, he attacks on many fronts. When he attacks physical health, there is the pain, then the diagnosis with the charts, and then the words from the physician. The feeling within your body, the proof you see with your eyes, and the words you hear from the doctor are the enemy's attempt to cause fear and hopelessness within you.

One Sunday morning many years ago, my wife and I were sitting in the balcony of the local church as the meeting was about to dismiss. The deacon of the week walked onto the platform and took his place behind the pulpit. He was about to give the benediction when an older man, probably in his seventies, began walking down the long center aisle toward the front of the church. Even with the large crowd, the church was quiet. All eyes were on the older gentleman.

Upon reaching the front, he spoke to the congregation. In a deep cracking voice, he said, "I've never gone to church much, but last week I did go to the doctor. He said that my disease was terminal and that there was no hope for me medically. The doctor said that my only hope was God. I thought that if God could be found, it must be in a church, so here I am."

31

While the doctor was not necessarily trying to be religious, he instinctively knew that there was a power that was greater than the physical reality of the man's situation. Even though he told the farmer that there was nothing he could do medically and that his body was going to die, he gave the man hope.

When the doctor gave his report to the farmer, the farmer had a choice to make. He could choose to focus on the statement from the doctor that said he would die, or he could focus on the statement by the doctor that there was hope in God. His decision at that moment would determine his destiny. To focus solely on the problem would be submitting to the fear of the future, but to seek God would bring hope.

The doctor unwittingly planted the seed for choice. Regardless of where the bad news comes from, there is always a choice. While impending destruction may appear visible on charts, graphs, and x-rays, the destruction itself has not been experienced yet. Likewise, the written Word of God revealed in your heart is the promise of your deliverance. The deliverance or the destruction are future. Faith and fear activate your future. Worry leads to fear and hope leads to faith.

Don't Accept the Evil Report

God used Moses to lead the Hebrews out of the bondage of Egypt and into the Promised Land. As they neared the land of Canaan that God had given to them, Moses was told to send one representative from each of the twelve tribes to spy out the land. Among these twelve spies was the son of Jephunneh from the tribe of Judah, whose name was Caleb, and from the tribe of Ephraim, the son of Nun, whose name was Joshua.

Moses gave the twelve spies specific directions. He told them to head south and go up into the mountains. From there they should spy out the land to see what the people in the land looked like. He wanted to know how many there were and if they appeared to be strong or weak. He also wanted them to find out whether the land was good or bad and if their cities were like strongholds. He further instructed them to determine whether the land was rich or poor and whether or not there were forests. He told the twelve spies to have great courage and to bring back some of the fruit from the land because it was the time of the year for grapes to be ripe.

So the spies did as they were told: they spied out the land from the Wilderness of Zin as far as Rehob which is near the entrance of Hamath. As they came up through the south, they came to Hebron and some of the other cities where the descendants of Anak were. Then as they came through the valley of Eshcol, they cut down one cluster of grapes that was so large it took two men to carry it between them on a pole. For forty days they spied out the land, then returned to give the report to Moses and Aaron and to all the congregation of the children of Israel.

They stood before the people and gave good news. They said, "The land truly flows with milk and honey." Then they displayed the grapes and the fruit they had brought back.

But then their report changed. They said the people who dwelt in the land were strong and the cities were large and fortified. It was a land of giants and the people who lived there made them feel like grasshoppers in their sight.

Then Joshua quieted the people and proclaimed that they should immediately go into the land and take it just as God had told them to do. There was great division. Ten of the spies spoke fear saying that taking the land was impossible. Two of the spies (Joshua and Caleb) proclaimed the promise of God. They said that the land God had promised, He was faithful and able to deliver into their hands. But the children of Israel believed the negative report. They believed in their hearts and confessed with their mouths that they could not go into the Promised Land because of the giants (Numbers 13-14).

Israel eventually moved into the Promised Land, but it was forty years later. The words spoken by those believing the evil report came to pass and none of them who were above the age of twenty at that time entered into the Promised Land. The ten spies who gave the evil report and all of the adults who believed it, died in the wilderness during the forty years. But Joshua and Caleb moved into the Promised Land with a new generation of Israelites. Joshua became the leader and Caleb inherited all the land of Hebron (Joshua 14:14).

Now this Old Testament story simply reveals and further amplifies a principle of faith and confession: what they believed and spoke is what they received.

When you are told that it is impossible for you to break free from the bondage of depression and despair, do not believe the evil report but believe and receive the fullness of the blessing that God has for you. What God has promised you, He is fully capable of having it come to pass in your life. But the spiritual key that unlocks the blessing is this: what you believe in your heart and confess with your mouth is what you will receive. Don't accept the evil report!

Long-Term Hopelessness

It is possible for people to have been hopeless for such a long time that hopelessness itself has become a way of life. The dreams of youth have vanished, and life has become endless days full of tasks and duties with every day like the day before. The expectation for tomorrow is just another day like the days that have passed. They are living the life they never thought they would live, but because they are blinded to the possibility of hope, they have become what everyone wants them to be. They function in society, doing what's expected and feigning joy. While everything looks normal on the outside, there is emptiness within. Once they have reached this state, they need a supernatural spiritual intervention. Because they don't recognize the state they are in, they don't seek deliverance.

But even in this state, deliverance is possible! The grace of God can outperform any deception that the enemy brings. It may seem that this darkness is impenetrable, but there is a spiritual truth that proves the opposite to be true: God is light, and light always overpowers darkness.

Darkness Has No Power Over You

I am the light of the world. He who follows me shall not walk in darkness, but have the light of life.

John 8:12

The presence of light causes darkness to leave. Where there is light, darkness cannot exist. When problems in your life seem to be pulling you down into the pit of darkness, then you must make the decision to walk in the light of God's promise to you. As you follow His light, the darkness will always dissipate because darkness is subject to the light.

Satan is the prince of darkness, but Jesus has already defeated him. The Bible even says that Jesus made a public mockery of him and defeated death (Colossians 2:15; Hebrews 2:14). Jesus has authority over darkness and He has given that authority to all who believe (Luke 10:19).

Remember this today. If you are a Christian and you are being attacked by darkness, darkness is not really the problem. The problem is lack of light. So let your light shine (Matthew 5:16). Greater is He (the Light) who is in you than he (the darkness) that is in the world (1 John 4:4). The bottom line is this: God is light, and according to Jesus, when we walk in His light, darkness has no power over us because light always overpowers darkness.

The Light shines in the darkness. And the darkness has not overpowered the Light.

John 1:5 (ICB)

The Source of Hope

Many years ago I knew a young girl who was talented, attractive, and who had typical teenage thoughts and dreams. Many times while alone, her thoughts would drift and she would think about her future. She daydreamed of a young man who would sweep her off her feet and treat her with respect. She envisioned having a life together with children and experiencing all the joys of motherhood and being a wife. While the dreams of her future were fanciful, she still held on to the hope that someday they would become reality.

As the years went by, everything didn't turn out as planned. Her handsome young prince turned out to be a womanizer and a liar. The young teenage girl with dreams was now a middle-aged single mom playing the role of father, mother, and provider for the family. Holding down two jobs, the teenage dream of a glorious future had now become the daily quest for survival. As each day passed, her hope faded and was replaced by despair and resentment. In moments of utter frustration, she cried out asking, "Why did God allow my life to be ruined? What's the purpose of continuing this meaningless existence?"

For some, Prince Charming never shows up, and the daily wait for the dream that never seems to happen becomes a burden within itself. And as the years pass, the questioning begins: "Why have I been ignored? What's wrong with me?"

All of these circumstances can be brought together with one thought. *Is there hope when things look hopeless? Is it possible that the impossible situation can become possible?* The answer is yes, it is possible, but it is only possible when hope is in the heart.

The key is to find hope, true lasting hope. There is only one ultimate source for that kind of hope, and it is found in the promises of God which are found in His book of promises, the Bible. As you spend time meditating on those promises, hope will move from the written promise into your heart. The result will be freedom from guilt and regret, and a vision of the glorious future that is available and waiting for you.

The Plan for Your Life

Before you were even born, God conceived a plan for your life. While you were in your mother's womb, He knew you, loved you, and desired the best for you. In the same way that earthly parents want the best for their children, God has hopes and desires for you.

> You watched me as I was being formed in utter seclusion, as I was woven together in the dark of the womb. You saw me before I was born. Every day of my life was recorded in your book. Every moment was laid out before a single day had passed.
>
> Psalm 139:15-16 (NLT)

God is a good father. You are His creation, and He loves you. He loved you so much that He sent His Son to die so that you would never die, but instead spend all eternity with Him (John 3:16). You must understand this reality. He died for you personally. He created you, He knows your name, and He loves you! God's plan for your future is good, and He wants prosperity, health, abundance, peace, love, and life for you. As a Christian, He lives inside of you (Colossians 1:27) and rejoices in your daily victories. Abundant life is a life full of hope, knowing that the goodness God has promised is just around the corner!

This is good news! Jesus specifically stated this good life was for now, in this present age. Over the years I have heard many preachers preach about heaven and the goodness of eternity. While it is true that we who are Christians have rewards and joy waiting for us in the eternal kingdom, we cannot ignore the words of Paul when He said the goodness does not start in the future, but starts now (Ephesians 1:21).

Hopelessness Is Relative

Throughout my life I have been blessed to travel extensively. It's interesting that cultures vary to such a degree. Likes and dislikes, family customs, traditions, and desires vary from nation to nation. In every nation I have seen wealth and poverty, peace and unrest, hope and hopelessness, but I have discovered that hopelessness is relative. Let me explain.

A few years ago while traveling through the Golan Heights in Israel, we stopped to have dinner at a Druze village. The food was ethnic and actually very good. They have a way of making a falafel that is unique from any other Mideastern culture. They were friendly and although we had a little bit of trouble communicating, their hospitality was very warm. While I was there, a young boy came in whose mother worked at the restaurant. He had lost one of his shoes and evidently could not remember where he lost it. The other shoe was still on his left foot. It was an old tennis shoe that, quite frankly in America, most people would have thrown away. She left immediately with a look of great concern on her face. I thought to myself, *When I get home, I would love to send this young boy a couple pairs of new tennis shoes.* But he was gone, along with his mother, and as I said earlier, our communication skills were lacking.

A few weeks later after arriving home, I made a trip to a local department store to pick up supplies. This store sold a wide range of items, including food, clothing, pharmaceutical supplies, and electronics. While I was in the department store, I stopped by the electronics department for a few minutes.

When I arrived, there was a boy who appeared to be seven or eight years old sobbing and lying on the floor. At first, it looked like it might be some type of medical emergency. As I looked toward the mother, she was shaking her head while looking back at me, feeling that she needed to give an explanation. She said, "His new video game came out today and the store has already sold out of all of them. He's just a little upset. He'll get over it."

As I looked at the boy and saw that he was throwing quite a temper tantrum along with his sobbing, my thoughts flashed back to the Druze village. While the point of despair of a child in the Golan Heights came as the result of losing an old worn out tennis shoe, the boy of the same age in America was distraught over having his $100 video game delayed a day or two. He was crying and kicking his feet on the floor while wearing new $200 tennis shoes that had lights built into them.

The point is this: the young boy in the Golan Heights felt despair over the loss of something that was a necessity for him to walk in the rugged terrain where he lived. The boy in the department store felt despair over the delay of receiving a gift that he didn't need in life, but was strictly one of his many toys. This shows us that not everyone becomes distraught or feels despair by the same circumstances. While one student may be desiring a snowstorm so they can stay home from school, on the same day another person may be desiring sunshine so they can go to work.

For this reason you cannot judge another person's hopelessness or despair by your own standards or perception. Hopelessness is relative. While you may not be able to understand why someone feels despair, you must always remember that perception is real to the person perceiving it. You can't judge or repair someone else's hopelessness based on what would solve your own personal problem. You may feel that they have allowed themselves to be deceived by someone or the circumstances and you may be right. But deception is never discerned by the one being deceived. That's why it's called deception.

Your Trial May Be an Illusion

Because of deception, there are times when hopelessness is only an illusion. There are times when things look bad, or appear hopeless, and even look impossible, but sometimes these looks are deceiving. Over the years there have been many times I have counseled with people who were in real mental anguish over something that had happened only to find out later that what they thought was true was not true. It is a reality that things are not always as they appear.

I remember the day Loretta, my wife, frantically called me at the office to tell me there was a man trying to break into our house. Actually, it was the bug exterminator just doing the job I had hired him to do, but Loretta didn't know that. Seeing the story from two different sides made me realize that although the person telling the story believes it to be true, things are not always as they seem.

At that time, I was working in our family marine business. We manufactured, sold, and serviced boats on the Lake of the Ozarks in Central Missouri. Because of the winding nature of the lake, the roads are not uniform in a grid as they would be in a city or a rural housing development. In order to get from one place to another on the lake, a person must travel a network of dusty, winding, narrow roads. My home was a waterfront home at the end of one of those eight-mile winding roads. We had no close neighbors. On one side of our house was the lake, and surrounding the house were hundreds of acres of forest.

Loretta was in panic mode when she called me that day. She told me that there was a man walking around on the deck of our house who appeared to be trying to break in. I could hear the stress in her voice. I did not know the exterminator was going to show up that day, so I was not aware of who the man was either.

I instructed her to hide in the bathroom in our master bedroom. The bedroom was on the second level with one complete wall being glass, facing the lake. This room, like all the other rooms, exited onto the deck. She told me she would hide, so I immediately jumped into one of the marina service trucks, grabbed one of my employees, and at a high rate of speed headed toward my house. Driving at normal speed, it was about thirty minutes away, although we did not drive at normal speed.

We were about five miles from the house when we met a vehicle heading toward us at lightning speed. I could see the panic on this man's face through the windshield. He didn't even slow down as we came around the corner barely missing each other, but sped on past throwing rocks at us with his tires. Thoughts were bombarding my head as I would not allow my mind to think what it was trying to think. I was praying fast and driving fast and believing that Loretta was okay. I knew in my heart the vehicle speeding past us was the man who had been at my house. I pulled up to the house and ran inside. I saw Loretta standing there, breathing heavily, but completely safe. I asked her what had happened, and the story began to unfold.

She had gone into the bathroom off of our master bedroom like I had told her to do. But after a few minutes of not hearing anything, she came out to look around. While she was in the bedroom, she heard the noise on the deck again, so she dropped to the floor to hide behind the bed. Underneath the bed she saw what looked like a handgun, but it was actually a BB pellet gun. She said when she saw that gun, something came over her. She grabbed the toy gun, stood up, and ran over to the outer wall. With her back against the outer wall, she could hear the man moving in front of the sliding glass door. As he got in front of the glass doors, Loretta leaped out from behind the wall and with a stance like a policeman at a target range, held the toy pistol (that looked real) on the man. He was so startled that he dropped everything in his hands and ran to his little pickup and drove as fast as he could away from our house. She described him and he was definitely the man we met on the road!

I walked out onto the deck to find the gun that the man had dropped when he left, but there was no gun there. All I could find was the insect termination equipment the man who was spraying our house for insects had dropped when he left in a panic because a crazy lady had pulled a gun on him. Her actions and his actions were both a result of something that was only perceived.

While this story is something we have laughed about for years, it reveals a bold truth. Everything that looks destructive may not be. What Loretta saw, she perceived to be a burglar. What the bug man saw, he perceived to be a crazy woman with a gun ready to shoot him. They were both wrong. Loretta learned the truth when I explained to her that I had hired the exterminator and that he had arrived without an appointment. The bug exterminator never did learn the truth because we never saw him again. He is probably still telling his grandchildren the story about the day he almost died!

When you take action based upon what you think you see, you can actually alter your life. Although Loretta's action was bold, had she known the complete truth, her actions would have been different. I knew I had hired the exterminator, but because I had not informed Loretta, she was not prepared. So many times what we see appears to be one way when, because of a lack of knowledge, it is actually another.

A lack of knowledge and understanding of God's plan for our life can create despair and wrong actions. In Hosea 4:6 God says, "My people are destroyed for a lack of knowledge."

Knowledge doesn't always come from what you see because sight is limited. You cannot see what is going on in someone else's heart. You cannot always believe what you hear from someone else's mouth; and the actions of others can only be measured visually. Only when we learn to walk by faith and not by sight will our actions be based on truth. Remember, faith is trusting God and His Word.

While the disaster in this story was totally perceived and there was no threat from either party, there are times when the threat is real, but God himself uses humor to solve the problem.

Laughter Changes Things

This was the case one day when my secretary at my office told me I had a call on line three that seemed very urgent. Because of the urgency of the call, I decided to take it even though I had two other calls on hold and people waiting outside my office to speak to me.

When I picked up the phone, the young man on the other end of the line began by telling me how much he respected me and how much of an influence I had been in his life over the years. Because he respected me, he thought that I deserved to have a call from him before he took his gun to kill himself. He told me that he was sitting in an easy chair next to a desk, and he was going to end his life when we got off the phone.

What I did that day I am not recommending anyone ever do. What happened was completely led by the Holy Spirit for that specific situation even though my mind was thinking, *Why am I saying this?*

As soon as he had finished telling me that he was going to kill himself when we got off the phone, I heard myself say to him,

"Look, I'm very busy today. I have two calls on hold and people waiting for me in the hall. I really don't have time to deal with this right now. You said in your own words that you respected me and that I have been a friend to you. If that's true, then I have something I would like to propose to you. I want you to take the bullet out of the gun. I'm sure you only have one bullet. If you are any shot at all, that's all you would need. Take the bullet out of the gun and put them both in your desk drawer, then give me two hours. It's four o'clock now and the office closes at six. I should have everything caught up by then, and I will return your call. When I do, I'll give you plenty of time to take the gun and the bullet out of the desk drawer, put the bullet back in the gun, and we'll take up where we are right now. Obviously you've waited forty-three years to do this. Can you just give me two more hours?"

I'm sure this is not what he was expecting to hear. It was quiet on the other end of the phone. He hesitantly said, "Well... I guess I could." I responded, "Okay, take the bullet out of the gun," then I waited until he did. Next I said, "Put the gun and the bullet in the drawer," and he did. I said, "I'll call you back at six," and he replied, "Okay I'll be waiting for the call," and we hung up.

Once again, what I am telling you is not a recommended course of counseling, but rather an historical account of what happened this one specific day under the leading of the Holy Spirit.

When six o'clock came, I gave him a call. When he answered the phone, I called him by name and said, "Now, I'm going to give you a couple of minutes. Get out the gun and the bullet, put the bullet in the gun, and we'll take up right where we left off."

I could hear him laughing on the other end of the phone, and he said, "No, I don't have to do that now. Everything is fine!" I asked him, "What happened?" He said, "When I got off the phone with you, I got to thinking about what you said about taking out the bullet and in two hours you would call me and we would take up where we left off. It just seemed so funny that I have been laughing for the last two hours!" He said, "Everything is fine. There are no problems now."

To this day, this young man has been living a happy life with his family. As I look back on this incident, I can hardly believe that it actually happened because it's not my nature to say something that bizarre in a critical situation that could mean life or death. But under the leading of the Holy Spirit, there are times when the unusual needs to happen. That day I discovered as a reality that laughter and a merry heart does good like a medicine, just as the Bible says (Proverbs 17:22).

The Joy of the Lord Is Our Strength

Sometimes when things look hopeless, in reality some of the perceived despair could simply be because we're taking some things way too seriously. While it is true that there are many situations that have no humor to them, we must never forget that the joy of the Lord is our strength (Nehemiah 8:10). Strength is needed in times of battle. The ability to laugh in difficult situations reveals at least a spark of hope from within. Of course, humor and joy aren't the same, but it is difficult to have humor if we have no joy.

Fighting the good fight of faith is a battle. But here's the good news: when we fight the good fight of faith believing and acting on what God says about us, we always win! No matter how horrible or desperate the situation may be, a little laughter, or something funny can completely change our outlook as it did for this young man. By getting his eyes off of what appeared hopeless, he saw things differently and his life was spared.

...The joy of the Lord is your strength.

Nehemiah 8:10

The Joy of Hope

These things I have spoken to you, that My joy may remain in you, and that your joy may be full.

John 15:11

There is joy, peace, and freshness that flows through us when we have hope. When our heart is broken, hope opens our eyes to allow us to see clearly the goodness that God has planned for us. When a person walks in hope, there is a snap in their step, enabling them to skip through the day with hope flowing over the skin and through the hair like a fresh breeze on a summer day. With hope in your heart, you cannot help but have a smile on your face knowing that greater is He that is in you than he that is in the world (1 John 4:4).

Hope brings an assurance that the problems of the past cannot keep you in bondage as you glide forward moving ever closer to the manifestation of the promise. With hope, there is an eagerness to awake in the morning to tackle the challenges of life, knowing that the challenges will be resolved. Hope is ever looking forward and not looking back. In fact, hope forgets those things that are behind and presses forward to the goal knowing that when attained, there will be refreshing (Philippians 3:13-14). Regardless of the joys of the past, hope knows that the best days are yet to come. As each new day becomes better than the previous day, hope strengthens knowing that there is no end to the expanse of joy.

Hope and joy are eternal. Not only does hope create an atmosphere of anticipating goodness to come, but hope itself becomes manifest with gratefulness and thankfulness. Hope is never prideful, but recognizes that deliverance comes through the Word and not through the flesh. Hope doesn't strive for fame and fortune, but if it is given, it is received with humility.

> **Brethren, I do not count myself to have apprehended; but one thing I do, forgetting those things which are behind and reaching forward to those things which are ahead.**
>
> **Philippians 3:13**

Get Your Hopes Up

One of the worst things that can be spoken to a person who is trying to stay above depression and despair is for a friend to tell them, "Don't get your hopes up." To the contrary, that's exactly what a person who is battling hopelessness needs to do. They need to get their hopes up!

But true hope cannot be found in the advice of worldly friends. Hope has its source in God's Word. Find the hope you need that is quoted in Scripture and surround yourself with godly people who know the truth and who will help you get your hopes up.

Chapter 3

False Sources of Hope

A feast is made for laughter, and wine makes merry; but
money answers everything.

Ecclesiastes 10:19

The wisdom of King Solomon is considered to be the greatest wisdom of the ages. Throughout the centuries, his sayings which are recorded in the Holy Bible have been quoted by
theologians and secular society alike.

An example of his wisdom is told in the book of 1 Kings.
King Solomon was presented with a problem of two mothers.
The one mother's son had died during the night. While the other
mother was sleeping, the woman took her dead son, switched
him with the living baby, and then claimed he was her own.
They were brought before the king who was to determine which
mother was the birth mother. In his wisdom, he commanded
that the baby be cut in two so that each mother would receive
half. One woman cried, "No! Give the other woman the living

child." When the other woman said, "Divide the child and give me my half," Solomon knew then which one was the real mother. He was truly gifted with God-given wisdom. (1 Kings 3:16-28.)

King Solomon was also the richest man on earth. His wealth and his wisdom were unequaled. It's interesting that near the end of his life, he said that everything was vanity (Ecclesiastes 1:14). But while everything was vanity, he also stated that money was the answer to everything (Ecclesiastes 10:19). How could this be? How can money be the answer to everything while at the same time it is vanity?

Shortly after his death, the wealth of his household was gone. Because the next generation did not walk in godly wisdom, the wealth was lost. However, his wisdom is still with us over two and a half millennia later. This gives us great insight into a spiritual as well as natural principle. Money is the answer to everything, but it is a temporary answer which only answers external things that we can see. But wisdom satisfies the heart and sustains itself eternally.

A Natural Example

Through my several decades of ministry, I can confirm that the lack of money has been a major source of family and marital issues. I have heard this statement countless times: "If I just made more money, my problems would be solved." In most cases, that statement is true. A certain amount of money would solve the problem. However, I have discovered that in most situations it is a temporary solution. While the statement of Solomon that money answers everything is true, usually after it gives the answer, it (money) quits talking and another answer is needed. The chase for money continues without true satisfaction in the heart. Money may give the answer for the moment, but in the end, as Solomon discovered, earthly riches are vanity.

Please don't misunderstand this statement. Solomon's wealth was not sinful. It was given by God, and God wants His children to be prosperous (Psalm 35:27) and not in poverty. But true riches (the fruit of the spirit listed in Galatians 5:22-23) will sustain you regardless of whether or not money is in your bank account. The apostle Paul said that he had learned to be content in whatever condition he was in (Philippians 4:11). Wealth or lack (external) did not affect his heart (internal).

Wealth Is Not the Source of Hope

Through countless hours of ministering to people who feel they have lost hope, I have discovered that whether wealthy or poor, the human heart only receives hope through believing the promises of God. I have seen multi-millionaires lose everything, and I have seen poor people who had nothing receive a windfall of wealth. While their circumstances may have changed for a short time, ultimately the condition of their heart did not change. Money does not change the heart.

It is faith that unlocks the promises of God in the realm of the spirit which allows them to flow into our daily lives. Faith is the substance of things hoped for. While it is impossible to have hope without true faith in God's Word, it is likewise impossible to have faith without Bible hope. They are power partners that work in tandem. When true hope and true faith connect, there is nothing that is impossible. Hopelessness and despair are like darkness. When the light of faith and hope are switched on, hopelessness and despair disappear.

Money Does Not Change Your Heart

Throughout my life I have been associated with the extremes of society. What I mean by this is that I have had friends who were dirt poor as well as friends who were excessively rich, but I have learned through observation that fame and fortune are irrelevant when it comes to issues of the heart. While the world places too much value on money, I have discovered this truth through the Word of God and by experience: Money only amplifies what is already in the heart. It does not change the heart.

Many times wealth is flaunted, especially by those who have recently obtained it. However, there are those for whom it is only an asset and not meant to impress others.

While working at our family marine business when I was younger, our family was involved in manufacturing as well as selling high performance power boats with twin and triple engines. These boats were beautifully detailed with an average cost of several hundred thousand dollars each.

It was during this time that a middle-aged gentleman, who could barely speak English, came into our store to have his boat serviced. It was a twenty-foot metal boat that had been painted several times, each time with a different bright color. Some of the paint had peeled off, revealing the previous colors. Needless to say, this boat looked like a building in the poor section of a third world country! The engine was old, but the engine, the boat, and the gentleman were always neat and clean.

He was an interesting man that everyone enjoyed talking to when he came in. Unlike some customers who had fancy boats, fancy cars, fancy clothing, $500 sunglasses, and an attitude, this man was pleasant. One day while talking with him, I asked him where he lived. Since our marina was in a resort area in the center of the United States, where most people traveled from urban areas to vacation at the lake, I was curious whether he came from Kansas City, St. Louis, or maybe even Chicago. He surprised me when he said, "I live in Central America." Then he began to tell me his story.

He was the owner of several coffee plantations and had houses in several resort areas around the world. He also had a jet with a full-time pilot who would fly him anywhere he wanted to go, anytime he wanted to go. He had so much money that money was never a factor in his decisions.

Had we not had the conversation we had that day, I probably would have never known about his wealth. This man lived in Central America and vacationed at the Lake of the Ozarks every weekend. His house was modest, his boat was modest, and his clothing was modest, but he was fulfilled.

His father had started the coffee plantation almost eighty years earlier. This man grew up with unlimited resources, but instead of allowing the resources to control him, he controlled the resources. Instead of buying what he could afford, he purchased what he wanted. He had found peace in his life.

Wealth without Peace

Another friend of mine was also a gentleman with great wealth. Once he purchased fifteen hundred stores in shopping centers all across the United States as a side venture. He bought a power boat worth hundreds of thousands of dollars for each individual member of his immediate family. He had multiple homes, airplanes, and traveled extensively.

One day I realized I had not heard from him for several months, so I gave him a call on his cell phone. When I asked him where he was, he said he had leased a ship in the Mediterranean that he had been staying on for the last month. The ship was so large that it required a crew of thirty to maintain it.

I asked him why he was cruising the Mediterranean. He explained that he just had to get away from everything because his son had died a few months earlier. When I gave him condolences and let him know that I would be praying for him and his family, I could hear the quiver in his voice as he replied that I was the first person to call him. All of the money, investments, stores, and employees had not helped him develop relationships. Evidently people saw him as unapproachable or possibly just a source of finances.

After praying with him and hanging up the phone, I heard the Lord speak to my heart about judging people based upon their wealth. We've often heard it said that Jesus died for the poor as well as the rich, but we must also realize that He died for the rich as well as the poor.

This brings us to the reality that money cannot buy hope. The source of our hope is the promises that come from God, not our financial status.

Money Is an Amplifier

Many people have been taught that money corrupts and creates bad character in a person. The reality is money is nothing more than an amplifier.

If a man who doesn't have a whole lot of money will take a woman to a cheap motel to commit adultery, lots of money or lack of money won't change his character. If this same man suddenly became rich, the only thing that would change is that he would fly the woman to a tropical island resort and commit adultery in an expensive hotel. His character won't change. The sudden riches just allow him to put into action the bad things already in his heart. Money doesn't change character; it just amplifies character.

If a good person without much money gives a few dollars to help the poor, then suddenly gets a boatload of money, their character will also be amplified. Instead of a few dollars, thousands of dollars will go to the poor. Money amplifies the character that is already within. Again, it doesn't change existing character.

The Bible never says money will corrupt. We have all heard people say that the Bible says money is the root of all evil. But that is not what it says! The Bible says, "The love of money is a root of all kinds of evil" (1 Timothy 6:10). The love of money is what is behind pornography, murder, and gambling. The love of money in the heart is the root of evil, but remember this: it's not the money that's evil.

Riches to Rags

For many people, pride is associated with wealth, and humility is associated with poverty. However, this is not necessarily true.

Several years ago, my wife and I had the privilege of having brunch with a friend and his wife who, at the time, was listed as one of the richest men in America. He was well known for his financial dealings and was the owner of a national sports franchise. After brunch, we had watched the nationally televised sporting event from his multi-million dollar suite. We had watched the game from the owner's suite many times before and also many times after; however, this day was different.

After the game, we were escorted out of the owner's suite to the private parking area. We left the stadium to spend the evening with another couple who were friends of ours. Our friends invited us to go with them to get dinner at a drive-through restaurant. So we all piled into their double cab pickup truck to head off to the 99-cent hamburger joint.

The truck was older and a little dusty because my friend had been hauling hay all day. A broom and a rake were stuck into the slots in the back of the pickup bed. On this warm evening, the windows were rolled down on the truck because it had no air conditioning. The straw was swirling around from the pickup bed into the back of the cab so by the time we pulled up to the drive-through window, we looked like hillbillies that had just walked out of the field.

That's when I realized that within a few hours on the same day we had gone from being surrounded by great wealth to the extreme opposite. Then I noticed something that has stayed with me from that day until now.

The people who were extremely rich never flaunted their money nor did they act prideful concerning it. Instead, their conversations centered around their desires and goals including what they wanted to accomplish in life. On the other hand, the couple who did not have much money talked about money constantly. Not only did they talk about it, but their conversation was continually drawn toward criticism of those who had money.

The truth I learned that day reaffirmed the reality that humility and a person's degree of wealth are not connected, but humility is directly connected to a person's ability to walk in the fruit of the spirit as well as to be led by the spirit.

The True Source of Prosperity

Throughout my life, there have been times when I've been "broke," but I've never been poor. Broke represents a lack of money, but poor is a condition that is internal. Broke represents what I don't have on the outside that can be seen. Poor represents what's on the inside. While there have been times when I didn't have enough money, I did not have a poverty mentality.

You may ask, "How can you be broke, without money, and not be poor? Not having money is the outward manifestation of poor people." The answer is quite simple. I believe what God says about me, instead of believing what appears to be my condition.

God's Word says that He supplies all my need according to His riches in glory (Philippians 4:19). That means my prosperity is linked to His riches and not to mine. How could I be poor when the Creator of the entire universe is the supplier of all my need? What appears to be a state of being poor is really only a temporary journey through the storm, because His prosperity is waiting for me when the storm clouds disappear.

If we see our prosperity as being connected to God's promise that He will be our supply (2 Corinthians 9:10), then our focus will be on Him rather than on our lack or abundance. And when we seek first His righteousness and His kingdom, then all the things we need will be provided.

> But seek first the kingdom of God and His righteousness, and all these things shall be added to you.
>
> **Matthew 6:33**

Do not allow the fear of money to develop within you. Many fear riches because they have been taught that riches affect your character. Your character is a result of the seeds you have sown in your heart and the proper focus of what you love. To have a true understanding of the peace and hope that God has for us, we must love what He loves and hate what He hates.

To believe that money can change your heart is to place money as an idol and something you worship. If money becomes your number one goal in life, then it becomes your god. When you place another god before the true God, you eliminate your source of true hope.

The Deception of Fame

If there was ever anything that we have learned from Hollywood, it's this: fame without true character based upon godly principles can never bring happiness. While fame with character can allow you to fulfill some desires in your heart, it can never replace the source of your hope that are promises from God. In the same way that it is an illusion and untrue that wealth has the power to bring hope, it is likewise impossible for fame to satisfy your heart and lead you to victory in your life.

Through the years and decades of my life, countless movie stars and musicians have needlessly taken their lives. In almost every case they left behind excessive fortunes and great fame. But even with fame, evidently there still remained an emptiness and brokenness that fortune and fame could not repair.

A great deception, especially among the young, is that fame itself will bring fulfillment and satisfaction in life. The Bible says that faith pleases God (Hebrews 11:6). But while fame is not bad in itself (it is a tool that can be used to influence people), it does not bring lasting peace to man, nor does it please God. Faith pleases Him, not fame. Fame is an illusion with no substance.

Many people who become famous find that their fame is superficial and discover that it only lasts for a short season. Sometimes their fame relies solely on their abilities and skills. This deception of fame sometimes starts in childhood. Sadly for many this immature action develops into an adult lifestyle. Let me explain.

In elementary and middle school there are children who have natural talents as well as good looks. Many usually end up being class presidents, cheerleaders, and stars of the most popular sports team at the school. Some of these young children are pushed into the limelight and develop a self-confidence that is attractive. In their school, these children are famous. Many times other students will do anything they can just to be seen with them or to talk to one of these popular students. To a degree, it's natural to be drawn to leaders and confident people. But all too often children will do anything to associate with those of popularity. This can be deadly if the character of the popular child is flawed.

While we see this trend in children, it should be avoided as we mature in life. Yes, we are all drawn to those of influence, but we should never submit our will to them. When I was younger, my mother asked me if all the other kids jumped off a cliff, would I? I remember thinking to myself, *It depends on which kid jumped.*

So the conclusion is this: it's the nature of mankind to be influenced toward the good or bad by the friendships we make. Fame, like money, is not evil, but can be used as a tool for good or evil. The Bible says that Jesus had great fame that spread throughout the region. He used His fame to draw the multitudes so He could preach the gospel to them. On the other hand, I have known of famous people who have used their fame to manipulate other people out of their fortunes. While fame is a tool, it should never be the goal.

Associations with Others

In the United States, I have noticed throughout the many presidential elections during my lifetime that conservative voters and liberal voters are both clustered into certain geographical areas. I used to wonder why the liberals moved to certain states or regions while the conservatives lived in other areas. The truth is this: geographical areas became liberal or conservative because of their associations. Likewise, the mind-set of community organizations and churches can influence the thinking of their communities.

Many decades ago, I was invited to a dinner party where I met several influential people. They were positive, polite Christians who became my friends. But there was something different about them that was unique from all my other friends. They each owned an airplane.

Although I always enjoyed traveling by air and watching the Blue Angels air show in Pensacola, Florida, I had never considered being a pilot and owning my own plane. But the continued association with my new friends, who were all pilots and owned their own private planes, caused the desire to build within me. It wasn't long until I had become a pilot with a beautiful plane (that I owned), sitting in a hangar (that I owned) at a local airport. Our associations with others throughout our lives truly affect our desires as well as our attitudes.

So what does all of this have to do with hopelessness and regaining hope? If things have pulled you down, if you are battling depression or insecurity, if your heart is broken, if you feel like all is lost, or if you feel like you are in a pit with no way of escape, the last thing you need is a negative speaking friend who lacks character and integrity to agree with you. You must find friends who think a little brighter, see a little further, and have more hope for their own life than you have for your own. The emotional pull of others must be in an upward direction!

When I was younger, I loved playing table tennis. I wasn't the greatest, although I did receive the first-place trophy in a tournament in Puerto Rico. I remember someone asking me what the key was to developing my "ping-pong skills." Instinctively I said, "I never like to practice with someone that I can beat. I always practice with someone better than I am."

That principle applies to so many things in life. If you want to have hope, find someone who has some! The Bible explains it this way. If you want to find a friend, you must show yourself friendly (Proverbs 18:24).

The True Source of Hope

As you have seen in this chapter, there are many sources of false hope. Unfortunately, some of them seem true. The Bible says that even Satan can transform himself into an angel of light (2 Corinthians 11:14). For this reason, we have emphasized greatly that God's promises to you are the source for your hope.

The physical things of life that you can see (fame, fortune, and earthly friendships) may appear to be the source of your hope, but they are not. It is true that God can use fame, fortune, and people to bring encouragement and guidance. But ultimately they are not your source and cannot bring the perfect peace and healing to your broken heart that you desire.

The only true source of hope is God's promises to you written in His Word.

Chapter 4

Healing Your Broken Heart

The Spirit of the Lord is upon Me, because He has anointed Me to preach the gospel to the poor; He has sent Me to heal the brokenhearted.

Luke 4:18

God understands what it's like to have a broken heart. In the beginning, God created the angels, but they were not like Him. Although they were beautiful and powerful, they were not created to satisfy the need for fellowship within God himself. So God created man in His own likeness and in His own image. God placed man in a beautiful garden called Eden and provided everything he needed to live forever. The fellowship that God and man enjoyed was like nothing that had ever been before. Their friendship was perfect until man secretly betrayed God and broke the relationship. God had done nothing wrong. He didn't deserve to be separated, but man chose to believe the lies of someone else. God understands betrayal that leads to a broken heart.

Because of the separation, man no longer walked in the glory of God but could only look back to the memory of how things were before. For man everything looked hopeless. But God had a plan.

We know that God loved mankind so much that He sent Jesus to reconcile the relationship that had been broken. The Bible tells us that not only did Jesus die for our sins so that we could have eternal life, but He also came to destroy the works of the devil and to heal the brokenhearted so that the reconciliation to God would be complete.

> **Now all things are of God, who has reconciled us to Himself through Jesus Christ.**
>
> **2 Corinthians 5:18**

> **For this purpose the Son of God was manifested, that He might destroy the works of the devil.**
>
> **1 John 3:8**

Of course, Jesus completed everything He was sent to do. The price for eternal life has been paid. The works of the devil have been destroyed and the healing of your broken heart has been accomplished. When Jesus said, "It is finished!" (John 19:30), He was saying that He had completed everything He was sent to do. Because Jesus completed the purpose of His mission, you can now walk in the fullness of a healed heart. Completing His purpose made it possible for you to have a life full of the joy and blessings you were created to have.

So, if Jesus came to heal the brokenhearted (which He did), and if He completed everything He came to do (which He did), then why is your heart still broken?

Don't Blame God

There might be many reasons that you are holding on to your broken heart. You may think God allowed your broken heart for a greater purpose or that He is punishing you for a past failure or sin. It could be that holding on to unforgiveness or offense is keeping you under the bondage of a broken heart. You may be deceiving yourself by not understanding the source of your pain. Perhaps you think God doesn't care, or you may simply believe a lie. But the truth is this: God desires you to be free from the pain of hurt, brokenness, and disappointment. He is not the source of your bondage, but He is the source of your freedom.

Years ago, I purchased a book by Kenneth E. Hagin entitled, *Don't Blame God.* After reading this book, a great spiritual truth was established in my life that can be applied to every trial and tragedy known to man. We cannot blame God for what the devil does. In other words, the truth is this: God is a good God, and the devil is a bad devil. God created man in His own image with the fullness of the blessing. The enemy, from the very beginning, has sought to destroy God's creation. The enemy is cunning, deceptive, and uses every method available to bring about this destruction.

Is It God or the Devil?

How can we tell if something is the result of the work of God or the work of the devil? As a pastor, I hear this question on a regular basis. However, all we have to do is look at the mission statement of God and the mission statement of the devil and then we can easily define the source. Both mission statements can be found in one verse: "The thief does not come except to steal, and to kill, and to destroy. I have come that they may have life, and that they may have it more abundantly" (John 10:10).

A mission statement can be described as a guideline to keep members and users aware of an organization's or leader's purpose. John 10:10 clearly defines what God does and what the devil does. It divides what they do into two columns. Everything that happens in life can be listed in one of these two columns. Let me explain.

The thief is your enemy. The thief represents Satan and his mission statement is to steal, to kill, and to destroy. But who is it that he wants to steal from? It's you! Who is it that he wants to kill? It's you! Whose life does he want to destroy? It's yours! And this is his desire for all of mankind. Satan is the prince of darkness, the father of lies, and the source of chaos, confusion, and destruction. Jesus said that he was a murderer and that there was no truth in him (John 8:44).

After Jesus stated Satan's mission statement, He proclaimed His own. Jesus clearly states His purpose. He came to give abundant life.

The mission statements are completely opposite. While Satan's purpose is death, destruction, and lack in our lives, Jesus came to bring life, restoration, and abundance.

So the next time you wonder if it is God or if it is the devil, ask yourself this question. Which column does "it" come under? If it steals in any way, if it brings death or leads to death, if it destroys or brings destruction, it's the work of the devil. If it brings abundant life full of *shalom*, it's the work of Jesus. Satan brings death. God brings life.

The enemy is the source of your broken heart. Jesus (the Word of God) is the only source who can "heal the brokenhearted and bind up their wounds" (Psalm 147:3). What you get depends on which source you choose.

Self-Deception

Deception is the enemy's greatest weapon in keeping a broken heart broken. Truth is God's weapon for healing a broken heart. Deception binds, blinds, and destroys. Truth frees, illuminates, and releases the captive from bondage. Deception by its very nature is deceptive but those who are deceived rarely recognize it. Why? They are deceived. Only knowing the truth can set you free (John 8:32).

The worst kind of deception is self-deception. When people have been deceived by someone else and they realize it, most deal with it swiftly and decisively. However, self-deception is a result of ignoring the truth while choosing to believe something that satisfies the flesh. It is rarely dealt with because someone who feels they are right often does not look inward.

The greatest depth of self-deception is when a lie that has been conceived is believed and embedded so deeply into the heart that no amount of logic or argument can dislodge it. The only thing that can defeat a falsehood is the truth. But when a person is self-deceived, many times they will not listen to the truth.

The Bible describes self-deception like this: "The way of a fool is right in his own eyes" (Proverbs 12:15). When pride enters into the heart of man, he is a candidate for self-deception.

Obadiah 1:3 states, "The pride of your heart has deceived you." You must examine yourself to eliminate deception.

Ways You May be Deceiving Yourself

You can deceive yourself and let hope be stolen by hearing the promise in the Word and thinking that simply knowing the promise will change things. You have to put action with it. Doing the Word means to act on what it says. You must believe what it promises to such a great depth that all of your speech, all of your actions, and all of your responses reflect the promise. That means if you hear and believe that Jesus came to heal your broken heart, and you believe that He accomplished what He came to do, then you will quit speaking and acting like your heart is broken.

> **Be doers of the word, and not hearers only, deceiving yourselves.**
>
> **James 1:22**

Another self-deception that allows hope to be stolen is thinking too highly of yourself, which is pride. Pride says that you can solve your problem yourself without any outside help, neither from friends nor from God. When you attempt to repair your broken heart yourself, you automatically exclude God, when in reality He is the only source of true repair.

> **For if anyone thinks himself to be something, when he is nothing, he deceives himself.**
>
> **Galatians 6:3**

Also, you can deceive yourself, allowing hope to be stolen by not acknowledging sin and by not repenting. Acknowledging sin is the first step in repentance. To *repent* means to turn around, to quit doing what you are doing and to do the opposite. When you refuse to acknowledge sin, you eliminate the need for repenting. Why? Because you feel nothing is wrong, so a change in direction does not seem necessary. Ignoring sin does not remove it, so when this becomes a lifestyle, the heart becomes hardened and repair becomes very difficult. A repentant and contrite heart is necessary for healing (Isaiah 57:15).

To heal the heart, it must be softened by receiving the Word. When sin is exposed, the decision must be made to repent. It is not automatic. It is a choice.

> **For sin, taking occasion by the commandment, deceived me, and by it killed me.**
>
> **Romans 7:11**

Another way you can be self-deceived is by placing your trust in the world's wisdom. The world's wisdom is better than the foolishness of the world, but the world's wisdom falls short of what is needed to permanently heal a broken heart. The wisdom of the world can come from many sources—friends, professional counselors, self-help books, etc. But while it may help superficially, it pales by comparison to the perfect healing that comes from the revelation of God's promises.

> **Let no one deceive himself. If anyone among you seems to be wise in this age, let him become a fool that he may become wise. For the wisdom of this world is foolishness with God.**
>
> **1 Corinthians 3:18-19**

You can deceive yourself by not bridling your tongue. A heart that is deceived will never grasp the truth. That is why you must be watchful not to let words fly out of your mouth when you are in an emotional state. It is easy to say things that you will later regret. These emotional words can cause great damage to your goal of gaining hope and healing your heart. In moments of despair, be careful not to devalue your own worth by saying negative things about yourself.

When tragedy strikes or an unexpected trial suddenly occurs, your first words are extremely important because they set the pattern for the words that follow. And the words that follow set the pattern for victory or defeat. To say things like, "Just when I thought things couldn't get any worse, this happened!" or statements like that do not build faith, but lay the groundwork for negative confessions. To speak faith with the words of your first response to a sudden situation takes training and effort because this goes against the natural way of thinking. The natural response is to say what you see or imagine, but the godly response is to speak words of faith.

> If anyone among you thinks he is religious, and does not bridle his tongue but deceives his own heart, this one's religion is useless.
>
> **James 1:26**

Not understanding the biblical principle of sowing and reaping can also bring self-deception. If you want hope, you must sow hope into others. In your friendships and associations, be the person who encourages and brings light into dark situations.

> Do not be deceived, God is not mocked; for whatever a man sows, that he will also reap.
>
> **Galatians 6:7**

Don't allow your hope to be stolen by thinking God doesn't care about you and your broken heart. He sincerely does care! Romans 8:32 says, "He did not spare even His own Son but gave Him up for us all" (NLT). Someone who doesn't care would not do that. First Peter 5:7 tells us to cast our care on Him, "for

He cares for you." Get rid of the thought that God doesn't care, because that is not true!

He heals the brokenhearted and binds up their wounds.

Psalm 147:3

There are many who live their entire lives with a broken heart because they mistakenly believe that their broken heart is a part of their contrition for past sins. In other words, they believe it is a never-ending payment for the sins of the past. Likewise, there are those who believe that God has allowed them to have a broken heart in order to humble them and keep pride from rising up.

Both of these assumptions are wrong, but are propagated by the lack of understanding as to the source of human suffering. Remember the mission statements in John 10:10. God is a good God, the source of life and things pertaining to life. The devil is deceptive, the source of death and destruction. Never allow yourself to accept something that is hurtful and destructive because you falsely believe it's from God. To do this will make you void of hope, submitting yourself to daily pain.

Do not be deceived, my beloved brethren. Every good gift and every perfect gift is from above, and comes down from the Father of lights, with whom there is no variation or shadow of turning.

James 1:16-17

Sometimes the seeds of self-deception are sown by "friends." While it is natural to associate with people like yourself, there are times when this can be devastating. Why? Because of the tendency for broken-hearted people to hang around with other broken-hearted people who wallow in their own self-pity. While the intentions of your friends may be to help you, many times they do the exact opposite. You must break free from the associations that are like you are, if you don't want to be "like you are." If your heart is broken, find an individual or a group that is full of joy and hope to associate with.

Do not be deceived: "Evil company corrupts good habits."
1 Corinthians 15:33

Why You Need to Forgive

Unforgiveness is like a cancer that grows deep within the heart. It remains undetected to the outside world, but it brings destruction. It is impossible to walk in the joy and freshness that hope brings when the poison of unforgiveness is sheltered beneath the surface. There is only one solution to eliminating this hindrance of your hope. You must forgive.

Many harbor their unforgiveness toward someone because they wrongfully believe that to forgive means they condone and accept the hurtful actions of the other person. Don't fall into that trap! Forgiveness does not mean that you condone the actions of the one being forgiven, and it does not mean that you must renew your friendship or become close to them. Why? Because forgiveness actually has nothing to do with them; it has to do with you and your heart. Forgiving someone doesn't change them or affect their relationship with God. It changes you and affects your relationship with God. Forgiveness cleanses your heart and allows you to receive hope.

The Healed Heart

Remember this: it is difficult for a person who is deceived to understand the depth of their deception. That's why it is so extremely important to surround yourself with godly friends who will lovingly guide you toward the truth. And this is the truth: deception of the heart must be eliminated for healing to begin.

There is nothing keeping your heart from being healed that you do not have the power to change, and it is the grace of God that empowers you to make the changes needed.

Why is it important for your heart to be healed and not broken? When the heart is healed with hope embedded into it, the result will be a manifestation of joy and expectancy. This hope empowers your faith and pushes back the kingdom of darkness that attempts to engulf you.

When you look at your broken heart, it may appear that the struggle for repair is too great or that the battle for victory is overwhelming. But never forget this: As you journey through life, there are many battles that must be fought. But the only fight the Bible tells you to fight is the good fight of faith (1 Timothy 6:12). Faith is believing God. As the battle for your heart is raging, you can rest in His promise knowing that when the battle is over, you will be standing in victory with a healed heart.

> The Lord is near to those who have a broken heart, and saves such as have a contrite spirit.
>
> Psalm 34:18

Chapter 5

What Are You Believing?

We can't have faith without hope, and we can't have hope without faith. They go together because faith is the substance of things hoped for and the evidence of things not seen. The reality is this: the unseen world is the real world, and this world we live in is the created world. God is the ultimate creator. He created what we see out of what we don't see.

> **We do not look at the things which are seen, but at the things which are not seen. For the things which are seen are temporary, but the things which are not seen are eternal.**
>
> 2 Corinthians 4:18

Why should you look at things that are not seen instead of things that are seen? Because the things that are seen are usually a problem. You see the debt, you see the sickness, you see the doctor's report, you see the problems of life that are all in the realm of the seen. God's Word says, "For the things which are seen are temporary..." Your problems, whether you see it that way or not, are temporary, *"...but the things which are not seen are eternal."* So the eternal world, which will be here forever, is the realm you cannot see now.

In the realm of the unseen is the solution to the problem you have here in the realm of the seen. God has the answer to your dilemma in the realm of the unseen. To be clear, your problem is here in the realm of the seen. The question is, how do you reach into the realm of the unseen to get the solution for the problem you have here on earth and bring the solution back to the physical realm where it will benefit you? The answer has to do with your confession.

What we say regulates what moves back and forth between the realm of the seen and the realm of the unseen. Hope and faith work together, but we have to understand that faith is a substance in the realm of the unseen. That substance called faith is the solution to the problem. That's why Paul said, when writing to the church at Corinth, that we must walk by faith and not by sight (2 Corinthians 5:7). What did he mean? He meant as Christians, we must live our lives based upon what God says instead of what we see. When His Word says one thing and our eyes see something different, then we must choose to act on His Word instead of our sight.

If you make decisions in life based upon what you see, you are going to have a life of chaos because you are going to live a reactionary life—a life where you are constantly reacting to something that is happening.

> **But if we hope for what we do not see, we eagerly wait for it with perseverance.**
>
> **Romans 8:25**

Delivered from the Power of Darkness

By faith we understand that the worlds were framed by the word of God, so that the things which are seen were not made of things which are visible.

Hebrews 11:3

In the physical world as well as in the spiritual world, hope is associated with light while hopelessness is associated with darkness. This should not come as much of a surprise because the physical world was created out of the spiritual world. The Bible says that what is seen was created out of what was not seen, so there is definitely a direct connection between spiritual light and physical light.

When a person is having a spiritual problem, it can be solved by running toward the light because God is light. When the light of God shines on a problem, all spiritual demonic manifestations and problems must go, because He has delivered us from the power of darkness.

He has delivered us from the power of darkness and conveyed us into the kingdom of the Son of His love.

Colossians 1:13

Darkness Is Subject to the Light

We know that light travels at the speed of 299,792,458 meters per second or 186,282 miles per second. That's faster than most people can comprehend. But let me ask you this. How fast does darkness travel? Darkness doesn't move under its own power. It has no light. Darkness retreats at the same speed that light advances. As we said before, darkness only exists where there is no light, because light always overpowers darkness.

The apostle John talked about light and darkness when he wrote, "In the beginning was the Word [referring to Jesus] and the Word was with God, and the Word was God. He was in the beginning with God. All things were made through Him, and without Him nothing was made that was made. In Him was life, and the life was the light of men. And the Light shines in the darkness, and the darkness did not comprehend it" (John 1:1-5).

The Greek word for *comprehend* (*katalambanō*) could also be translated as *overpower*. In that case, verse 5 would read like this: "And the light shines in the darkness and the darkness did not overpower it." Once again, we see that darkness is subject to the light.

With that in mind, remember that Jesus said in Matthew 5:14, "You are the light of the world." And He said in verse 16, "Let your light so shine before men, that they may see your good works and glorify your Father in heaven."

At the entrance of every house there is a light switch. When you flip the switch, the light comes on and the darkness goes away. But have you ever noticed that when you leave the room, there is not a dark switch that you flip to turn on the darkness as you leave? Of course not! To bring darkness back into the room, you turn off the light because light rules over darkness.

In the light is deliverance. In the light is the power to heal. In the light is the anointing and the manifested power of the Word of God. When you walk in the light and speak His Word from your heart, you receive restoration and healing. When you believe His Word and speak His Word in spite of what you see, that's called walking by faith. You receive your deliverance according to your faith.

According to Your Faith

Then He touched their eyes, saying, "According to your faith let it be to you."

Matthew 9:29

In Matthew chapter nine, Jesus touched the eyes of two blind men who were following Him and He healed them. Notice He didn't simply say to them, "You are healed," but instead He said, "According to your faith let it be to you." Another version of the Bible says, "As you have believed, so let it happen" (NTE). Where was the responsibility in this situation? It was on the ones who were blind and what they believed.

Jesus touched their eyes; He met them at their point of faith. They had faith that if He would touch them, they would be healed. Then when He touched them, according to what they had believed, it happened. That tells me it's really important what we believe. It is impossible to have vision without light. Jesus literally delivered them from the power of darkness.

Once when Jesus was in Capernaum, a Roman soldier, a centurion, approached Him and pleaded with Him. He told Jesus that his servant was at home paralyzed and in great pain. Immediately Jesus replied that He would go to his house to heal his servant.

Surprisingly, the centurion told Jesus that he was not worthy for Jesus to enter his house, but he offered another solution. He told Jesus that if He would just speak a word, his servant would be healed and explained why this would work. He said that like

Jesus, he had soldiers under his authority and if he told them to go or to come, they would do exactly as he commanded.

When Jesus heard him make this statement, He turned to His disciples and those following Him and made a profound statement. He said, "Assuredly, I say to you, I have not found such great faith, not even in Israel!" (Matthew 8:10).

It's amazing that of all the rabbis, Pharisees, teachers, and even His own disciples, Jesus declared that this Roman centurion (a Gentile) had more faith than anyone else in all of Israel. (Matthew 8:5-10.)

What did the centurion understand that caused Jesus to proclaim he had great faith? He understood submission and authority. The centurion said, "Send the word and my servant will be healed" (vs. 8). He didn't say, "Go touch my servant."

On the other hand, the blind men believed that if Jesus touched them, they would be healed. That's where they had focused their faith. He said to them, "As you have believed, let it be done unto you," and He touched their eyes and they were healed.

The centurion said to Jesus, "Speak a word, and my servant will be healed." Jesus said to him, "Go your way; and as you have believed, so let it be done for you" (vs. 13). Did Jesus go to his house? No, He didn't need to, because the centurion believed that if the word was sent, his servant would be healed. As he believed, it was done to him.

Let me ask you something. What are you believing? What you are believing is extremely important because the paradigm set in the Word of God is this: what you believe is what you receive. This clearly explains the words of Jesus when He said, "According to your faith let it be to you" (Matthew 9:29).

'Why Are You Afraid?'

There was a day when Jesus got into a boat with His disciples in Galilee. He told them that He wanted to cross the lake to the other side. The other side was the region of the Gadarenes.

While on their way across the Sea of Galilee, a storm arose and the boat began to fill with water. His disciples were in great distress and for a short time couldn't find Him. When they did, He was in the back of the boat asleep. They cried out to Him, "Lord, save us. We are perishing!" Jesus got up and rebuked the wind and the sea by speaking to it and saying, "Peace, be still." The wind ceased and the sea became calm.

Then He turned to His disciples and asked them two interesting questions. First, He asked them, "Why were you afraid?" and then before they could answer, He asked them the second question: "How is it that you have no faith?" Essentially He was asking them, "What were you believing?" It was obvious they were neither acting upon what He had promised them nor what He had taught them. If they had believed Him, there would have been no fear. They could have used the authority they had been given to calm the storm themselves. They spoke what they believed and said, "We are perishing." Because they believed what they said, they were in fear. Had they only believed the Master, there would have been no fear. (Luke 8:22-25.)

The Naked, Demon-Possessed Man

From there they sailed to the Gadarenes on a calm sea. As Jesus got out of the boat, a naked, demon-possessed man cried out before Him and started screaming, "What do I have to do with you, Jesus, Son of the Most High God? I beg you, do not torment me!" This man had been living among the tombs and had been demon-possessed for a long time. Because this man had been seized by demons many times in the past, he had been bound with chains and shackles. But his strength was so great that he would break loose and the demons would drive him into the wilderness, naked and crazed.

Jesus asked him, "What is your name?" and the man spoke and said, "Legion." He said this because he was possessed by many demons. Those demons begged Jesus to not send them into the abyss, but to permit them to enter into a herd of swine which was nearby. He did so and the demons went out of the man into the swine. But the demon-possessed herd ran violently to a steep place where they fell into the lake and were drowned.

When the people of the community came out to see what was happening, they found the formerly demon-possessed man sitting at the feet of Jesus, fully clothed, and in his right mind. It would seem that this would greatly please the people, but instead they were afraid. In fact, they were so greatly afraid that they asked Jesus to leave and depart from them. (Luke 8:34-37.)

As He was getting into the boat to leave, the formerly demon-possessed man begged Jesus to let him go with Him, but Jesus gave him a command and said, "Return to your own house, and tell what great things God has done for you." Evidently, that's exactly what the man did, because when Jesus later returned to the region of the Gadarenes, a great multitude was waiting for Him and welcomed Him. The deliverance that took place in one man changed the hearts of the people toward Jesus in an entire region. (Luke 8:38-39.)

Remember this: as your deliverance takes place, of course it is for you personally, but it could also be used as a testimony to others so that you could turn the hearts of an entire region towards Jesus. So don't internalize your deliverance or keep it a secret. Make it a testimony.

The Twelve-Year-Old Girl

One of the people waiting for Jesus was Jairus, who was a ruler of the local synagogue. Evidently, he was so impressed with what he heard about Jesus as a result of the witness of the man who was delivered, that he fell at Jesus' feet and begged Him to heal his only daughter, who was dying. She was twelve years old. Jairus said, "Come lay Your hands on her that she may be healed, and she will live."

As Jesus and Jairus left to go to his house, a multitude of people thronged Jesus, pressing in and making it hard for Him to travel. There was a woman in this crowd who had a flow of blood for twelve years. It's interesting that her sickness began the same year Jairus' daughter was born. She pressed through the crowd and touched Jesus' garment. Jesus immediately felt the release of power go out from Him, so He turned around in the crowd and asked, "Who touched My clothes?"

His disciples were confused at this statement because so many people were pressing in, and they couldn't understand why He would say, "Who touched Me?" But He ignored them and looked at the woman who told Him the complete story of how she had been ill for twelve years. She had spent her entire fortune on doctors, but had grown increasingly worse. She heard about Jesus and had started confessing by saying, "If only I may touch His clothes, I will be made well." At this point, Jesus made a very profound statement to her. He said, "Daughter, your faith has made you well. Go in peace, and be healed of your affliction."

In other words, He was telling her that what she believed and confessed is what she received. (Luke 8:43-48.) What are you believing?

While Jesus was speaking to the lady who had just been healed, a group who had traveled from Jairus' house found Jairus and said to him, "Your daughter is dead. Why trouble the Teacher any further?" When Jesus heard what they said to Jairus, the ruler of the synagogue, Jesus said to him, "Do not be afraid; only believe."

As Jesus traveled to the house of Jairus, He only allowed Peter, James, and John, the brother of James, to go with Him. These three men were in His inner circle because they were the closest to Him of all the disciples. As He approached the house, there was a great commotion and many were weeping and wailing loudly. Jesus asked them, "Why are you making all of this commotion and weeping? The child is not dead, but is just sleeping." Of course, they ridiculed Him, so He put them all outside the house. Then He took the father, the mother, and His three friends, and they entered the room where the child was lying. Jesus took her by the hand saying, "Little girl, I say to you, arise." Immediately, she got up and started walking. Those with Jesus were overcome with amazement. (Luke 8:49-56.)

So here's the point: when Jairus received word from those who had traveled from his house that his daughter was dead, he had a choice to make. Would he believe what he had been told by his friends and family or would he continue to walk with the Master and believe what the Master said—that his daughter was not dead, but only sleeping? He didn't send Jesus away, but continued with Him to his house, so obviously his hope was with the words of Jesus. He received what he believed. What are you believing?

The Most Unlikely Gospel Preacher

Once again, I would like to emphasize an often overlooked reality. As you receive deliverance, there can also be collateral deliverance. In other words, your freedom can help set other people free.

The formerly demon-possessed man was an extreme case. He ran through the tombstones at night terrorizing the entire region. They tried to restrict him with chains, but he broke every chain they put on him. Besides that, he was naked. He was probably the most unlikely candidate to become an influential gospel preacher in their entire community. So when he got delivered of the demons, and was clothed and in his right mind, his testimony spread like a shockwave throughout the land.

Remember that the multitudes following Jesus, the healing of the woman with the issue of blood, and the daughter of Jairus being raised from the dead were all a result of the testimony of one extremely delivered man.

How Do You Change
What You Are Believing?

There have been several times in my life, and it still happens occasionally, when I will receive distressing news late in the evening. Even though by nature I am a calm person, these words of discouragement or bad news can linger and affect my sleep that particular night. As a result, I have discovered a way of overpowering the bad news of the day so that I can receive a good night of sweet sleep.

What I do is this: at bedtime, I turn on my television to video recordings of great faith teachers like Kenneth E. Hagin,

Charles Capps, or T.L. Osborn. Then I set the timer for an hour or so and go to sleep listening to the Word of God being taught by a minister I trust. When I do this, I sleep well. Sometimes I wake up the next morning knowing something in my heart that I didn't know the night before when I went to sleep. Most sleep therapists agree that we can learn while we sleep, so it's imperative to go to sleep with the Word of God to build your hope as you dream.

> **So then faith comes by hearing, and hearing by the word of God.**
>
> **Romans 10:17**

We have established by the Word of God that our deliverance is directly connected to our faith, which is the substance of what we hope for and becomes a reality in our lives when we believe and act on it. As we read, hear, meditate, and confess God's promises, our faith will increase and our hope will grow.

Remember, as you cling to your hope without wavering, the solid foundation of faith will form under you, allowing you to stand strong and withstand the attacks of the enemy. As you walk on the solid foundation of faith, holding onto your hope, your joy and peace will automatically increase, stress will dissipate, and your deliverance will be realized.

Chapter 6

Imagine That

Imagination is an important part of faith. If you can conceive it in your mind, then you will begin to believe it. When you believe it in your heart, you will confess it and receive it. You must be able to visualize the promise of God in your mind's eye. While it is true that "we walk by faith and not by sight" (2 Corinthians 5:7), you must remember that this biblical truth is referring to physical sight and physical senses. You must walk according to the promise of God but to do that, you must be able to imagine and visualize His promise coming to pass.

I heard a story of two great men of faith who were riding together in a car. As they were driving, they passed a large mansion off in the distance. It was a beautiful home that looked large enough that maids and butlers would be needed to keep it running. The yard was massive and well-groomed with beautiful trees and shrubbery. When one of the ministers saw this beautiful estate, he spoke these words: "I can't imagine living in a house like that." The other minister instinctively made this statement: "You don't have to be concerned about it. You never will."

Why would he make such a statement? It's because if he couldn't imagine it, then he couldn't believe for it. We only receive what we believe and without belief there is no faith.

> **God, who quickeneth the dead, and calleth those things which be not as though they were.**
>
> **Romans 4:17 (KJV)**

I call this biblical principle "calling those things that be not as though they were." What this means is simply this: you speak the promise that you don't see physically as though you do see it physically. But in order to do this, you must visualize it first as a completed promise in your mind. Otherwise, you will never speak it from your heart.

At creation, God spoke and commanded, and all of creation came into existence. He knew what He wanted and although it didn't exist physically, it did exist in His mind. Then He spoke it and it came to pass.

Can You See?

I recently heard the testimony of a woman who was legally blind and wore glasses that were as thick as the bottom of a Coke bottle. She had been prayed for many times by many different ministers, always with disappointing results to the point she didn't want to be prayed for again. A healing evangelist came to her church, and on the last night of the meetings, he called for her to come and receive prayer. She reluctantly left her seat and walked to the front of the church.

The minister asked her if she wanted to regain her sight. "Of course!" she replied. He said to her, "Take off your glasses. I am going to pray for you, and then I want you to tell me if you can see." So he laid his hands on her and prayed for her, then said, "Now, can you see?" She started to open her eyes, and he said to her, "Close your eyes! I didn't tell you to open your eyes!" So she closed her eyes. He said to her, "Can you see now?" Again she started to open her eyes. This time he said to her, "I did not tell you to open your eyes! Close your eyes and don't open them. You've got to see yourself seeing before you can see."

The woman was beginning to understand what the minister was asking her to do. So she kept her eyes closed and began to see herself seeing in her mind's eye. She took the time to imagine what it would look like for her to be able to see. Then she opened her eyes, and her eyes were completely healed. She could see!

Visualizing the Completed Work

When I was young, there was a time when I thought I would like to be an artist. In pursuit of this, I enrolled in and attended one of the nation's premier art institutes. On the first day of my oil painting class, the instructor gave what he felt was his most important guideline and principle for being an artist. He said before your brush touches the canvas, you must be able to see your completed work. He went on to say when you look at the blank canvas, you must be able to visualize what you are going to paint.

While this may be a basic principle for an artist, it also reveals a spiritual truth. When God promises freedom from the bondage of hopelessness, we must be able to look at the canvas of our hope that has not yet been painted and see it as a finished work. Without a vision, the paint will go on the canvas randomly resulting in confusion (Proverbs 29:18 KJV).

Can You Imagine It?

Recently, I was talking with a lady in my church about her husband who needed healing. When I asked her if she could imagine him being well and returning to normal life, I could see a look of astonishment on her face. She was having a new thought. She said, "My goodness! I just realized I could not see him healed. I've been trying to do everything I thought I was supposed to do, but in my mind, all I could see was him dying or staying in the condition he is in. When it really came down to it, I could not imagine him being well. I just couldn't imagine it! I didn't even realize that I couldn't imagine it until you asked me."

This lady realized she was not using her God-given ability to imagine or visualize victory. Although we are created with the capacity to visualize victory and success, the enemy tempts us to visualize defeat and failure and he uses the physical senses to do this. If you will observe children playing, you will see that they have been born with the amazing ability to pretend and to make-believe. They imagine themselves flying and being super heroes, or pretend they are a princess living in a castle. They have extremely creative thoughts and ideas. This ability is God-given.

When we are young, we have so many dreams, plans, and possibilities of what can take place in our life. But for many, the ability to dream, or to even imagine something, doesn't seem to exist anymore. Because of the continual disappointment of not seeing dreams fulfilled or watching other people step on their dreams, the ability is hidden. The truth is, we are never beyond hope. God has placed within us the ability to dream for victories as well as success in life.

If you believe you no longer have the ability to dream, the truth is that ability is still there, but it is just covered up or weighed down and hidden by all of the hurts and disappointments of the past. As you learn to forgive and forget those things that lie behind and press forward, you will uncover and release your ability to dream. Then it simply becomes a decision. Will you dream about victory, imagine victory, visualize it in your mind, and allow the joy of hope to flow through you? Or will you decide to not think on these things, but rather dwell on the possibility of defeat, which only brings worry and discouragement that further covers up your ability to imagine?

A true confession from the heart is not possible without the imagination and visualization of the victory that is promised in the Word.

Imagination and Visualization Becoming Realization

Many years ago, I knew of a young girl who attended college with my sister. The girl's hometown had a festival every year. The main promotion was giving away a new car that a local dealership supplied. The local businesses gave away tickets from which the winner would be drawn randomly on the night of the festival.

My sister's friend needed a car and somehow it was born inside her that she was going to win this car. As she would see it being driven around town, she would think to herself, *That's my car!* It was a bright red, brand new car and the promoters had a big sign attached to the top promoting the event. She would think, *I hope they are taking care of my car and the sign doesn't scratch the paint!* She had conversations with other people telling them she was going to win it, to which they would reply back, "No you aren't. I'm going to win!" Obviously, they didn't believe either one of them would actually win it. But the girl saw herself driving it. She imagined it sitting in her driveway. She could see herself taking the car to college.

The night of the big event finally came. The event host gave all the tickets a final spin in the big tumbler before reaching in and pulling out the winning ticket. Someone's life was going to change in a moment. But who was it? Did all those months of seeing it, imagining it, believing it, and speaking it result in receiving it at that moment?

It did! The girl's name was on the winning ticket and that night her faith became sight. She actually did drive the car home, parked it in her driveway, and drove it to college. In the end, her imagination and visualization became realization.

The New Age Counterfeit

The New Age cult stole the principles of imagination and visualization from the Word of God and perverted them into a false doctrine. From the days of Adam and Eve until today, the tactic of the enemy has been to take pieces of truth that God has spoken and mix it with principles that dilute, confuse, and deceive. They reveal a way that looks right, but in the end it leads to destruction (Proverbs 14:12). Although imagination and visualization are spiritual principles, they are only proper to use when attached to the will of God that is expressed in the good things He has promised in His Word.

The enemy has taught that anything you can imagine or visualize can be yours and is completely detached from anything godly. The flaw in this principle is that man is encouraged to realize his personal fantasies and desires of the flesh without regard to God. Because New Age thinking builds upon these principles incorrectly, much of the church has ignored them completely out of fear. Too often some religious leaders have completely ignored the true principles of God because the enemy has highjacked and distorted them. We should never ignore the true operation of godly principles because someone else is operating in these principles falsely.

Can you imagine someone discovering that there are counterfeit dollar bills being passed around in the community? Then because of this, they discard and throw away all of their dollar bills, not knowing whether they are counterfeit or not? Of course, not! That's ridiculous! You never throw away what is good because bad exists.

Therefore, we must never discard the true principles of the Word of God because someone else is using or teaching them incorrectly.

> There are some who trouble you and want to pervert the gospel of Christ. But even if we, or an angel from heaven, preach any other gospel to you than what we have preached to you, let him be accursed.
>
> Galatians 1:7-8

Believe You Have Received

> Therefore I tell you, whatever you ask for in prayer, believe that you have received it, and it will be yours.
>
> Mark 11:24 (NIV)

In this verse, Jesus proclaimed the biblical principle of calling those things that be not as though they are. He said that when you ask God for something, you must believe you have already received it, and after you believe you have received it, then you will receive it. Of course, in order to believe it, you must first conceive it and see it mentally. It is virtually impossible to believe for victory without mentally seeing it first.

That's what believing in the heart and speaking out of the abundance of the heart is: speaking what you are seeing inside. The true power of the spoken word is when your heart believes what God has told you. When your heart believes, the natural result is that you mentally see the promise and you instinctively speak the promise. When Jesus said "Out of the abundance of the heart the mouth speaks" (Matthew 12:34), He was revealing to us how faith is activated and the promise is realized.

Now there are those who will take this principle and attempt to believe for things that God has not promised. This is where the full Word of God must be taken into consideration. In other words, scripture is proved with scripture.

First John 5:14 says if we ask anything according to His will, He hears us. The next verse says that when we know He hears us, then we receive what we have asked. So you can see by this verse that He only hears us when we ask for things that are according to His will. This means the principle in Mark 11:24—believing that you have received and then you will receive—is based upon the condition of 1 John 5:14 that what we ask must be according to His will. In other words, God grants our requests when we believe we have received what He has promised.

The Hope Killer Called Worry

Therefore, do not worry...

Matthew 6:34

When you imagine and visualize the glorious victory God has promised you, the result is positive hope for the future that changes the way you act and the way you talk. When you imagine and visualize possible defeat and disaster because of the way things look on every side, the result is negativity, worry, despair, and dread for the future. As a result, the way you act and the way you talk is filtered through fear and dread. When these negative imaginations become fully developed, hope is pushed away and replaced with the by-product of fear called worry.

One of the most prominent killers of hope is worry. Worry takes many different forms. Most people who are depressed have lost hope because they have listened to and believed the lies of the enemy. Depression could be called *anti-hope*.

Worry is negative, and it will make you think things are going bad whether they are or not. Worry will create stress and affect you physically. Worry paralyzes. It keeps you from doing what you need to do because you are too worried to do anything. Worry is not of God. It will steal your hopes and dreams and keep you from moving forward. When you worry, it reveals that you are not in faith, but actually in fear.

The Misconception of Worry

I knew of a mother who thought that if you really cared about your children, you would worry about them. She believed if you didn't worry, then you must not care and you would not be a good mother. Because this lady believed this, she spent much of her life fretting and worrying about her children. Sadly, this concept spilled over into other areas of her life, so she worried about anything she loved or was involved in. To her, this revealed her dedication.

Unfortunately, her misguided belief created much pain in her life when she could have been at peace. When things were going bad, she worried because they were bad. And when things were going good, she worried that they would go bad. Worry was woven into the fabric of her existence. It became her way of life.

Not only is that a horrible way to live, but worry takes us closer to fear by every word that comes out of our mouth. In the Bible, it's interesting to note that when Job encountered the disasters upon his life, he said, "The thing I greatly feared has come upon me" (Job 3:25). Again, worry leads to fear and fear involves torment and destruction (1 John 4:18).

Another time a person told me that he worried as protection. The individual said, "If I worry about how bad things could be, then when things don't turn out that bad, I feel relieved. But if things do turn out as bad as I worried, then I'm not as devastated because it was what I expected." There is a clinical word for this attitude – *dumb!*

Some people feel that they have no control over worry. I have actually had people tell me that the only way they could quit worrying would be if God would just take it away. Well, don't expect God to do it. It's your responsibility. Some things are spiritual and some things are of the flesh, and of course, they must be dealt with accordingly. However, let me say this. Worry always results in a manifestation of the flesh. What I mean is this: Jesus did not tell us to cast out worry. He said, "Don't do it." He said, "Do not worry." He told us to take care of it.

In Matthew chapter 6, Jesus preached His famous Sermon on the Mount. This sermon has a tremendous amount of teaching in it, but there is one thing that is often overlooked: Jesus commanded us, over and over again, not to worry.

For instance, Jesus said in verse 25, "Therefore I say to you, do not worry about your life, what you will eat or what you will drink; nor about your body, what you will put on. Is not life more than food and the body more than clothing?" Jesus continued saying, "Which of you by worrying can add one cubit to his stature? So why do you worry...? Therefore do not worry, saying, 'What shall we eat?' or 'What shall we drink?' or 'What shall we wear?'" (Matthew 6:27,28,31).

Then we come to the well-known verse, Matthew 6:33, where Jesus said, "But seek first the kingdom of God and His righteousness, and all these things shall be added to you." Usually when we read this verse we stop there, but we shouldn't. In the original Greek language, there is no punctuation. The periods, commas, and other punctuation marks were added by the translators. With that in mind, let's not quit reading with verse 33. Jesus said, "But seek first the kingdom of God and His righteousness, and all these things shall be added to you, therefore do not worry" (vv. 33-34).

Throughout Matthew 6, Jesus said over and over again, "Do not worry." Was He trying to make a point? Definitely!

Dwelling on, focusing on, and worrying about the problem, whether real or perceived, whether seen or not seen, only intensifies and enables the spirit of fear to bring the problem to pass. We must eliminate the worry that is caused by looking at a possible future problem. We do this by looking at the promise of future deliverance and letting hope have its perfect work in bringing peace to our hearts.

Hope or Worry Is Your Choice

Worry and hope are opposites in most ways, but they are similar in these distinct attributes: they are both unseen and have yet to come to pass. Worry is a by-product of fear and fear usually involves an impending disaster that as of yet is unseen. Hope expects to see the goodness of God in the land of the living (Psalm 27:13).

Through more than two decades of being the pastor of a growing church, I have counseled with many who were concerned about an event or action that had not yet taken place. In other words, they were fearful of something that they had not yet seen. Their worry about a possible future destruction caused depression, anxiety, and illness. It affected their family and their friendships. Because they were focused on their worry and because it was at the forefront of their thinking, it became the subject of all their conversations. Consequently, their friends avoided them.

Worry and fear are the exact opposites of hope and faith. Worry and hope look forward into the future and anticipate an impending disaster or blessing. Fear and faith are the substances in the realm of the spirit that activate what is being anticipated. When we believe the promise of God and believe His promise is on its way, we are in hope. When we don't believe God and His promises, but instead believe there is no hope, we are in worry. Anticipating the promise of God is hope. Anticipating the problems of the world is worry. When this belief about a future event becomes established in the heart, the result is faith or fear.

Where worry exists, the ability to imagine victory does not. Worry and the visualization of victory cannot co-exist because worry is the visualization of defeat. Worry is imagining defeat. Worry is seeing everything going wrong. Godly imagination is seeing everything go right and expecting it. That's Bible hope. While the imagination of expecting everything good coming to pass is hope, the imagination of expecting everything bad coming to pass is worry. Worry is a time waster, time killer, hope destroyer, and sleep stealer. Hope leaves you with peace and the ability to rest, even in a storm (John 16:33). Worry or hope is your choice.

What Are You Hoping For?

I've heard people say, "I've read the Scriptures, made confessions, and prayed, but I can't imagine being delivered and set free. In my mind, I think this is the way it's going to be for the rest of my life." Sadly, if that is what you are seeing in your mind's eye, you're probably right. But even though that's what you've been thinking, it does not have to be your destiny. There is hope. You can change your destiny, but the first step is to make the decision to change what you are thinking.

What you think is a choice. It is a choice that takes place in the realm of the soul. What you think or don't think cannot be blamed on anyone else. This is a step in the process of building faith, and you are in complete and total control of what you think. It is very refreshing to know the choice is totally yours.

One time a young man who was having bad thoughts asked me how he should handle them because, "After all," he said, "we all know you can't control your thoughts." Sadly, that's what many people think. But the truth is, that's a lie. You can control your thoughts.

The Bible clearly tells us what to think and what not to think. It tells us that whatever is true, noble, just, lovely, whatever is pure and of a good report, think about these things (Philippians 4:8). Another place it tells us to cast down and take captive every argument and thought that rises up against the knowledge of God (2 Corinthians 10:5). Again, God's Word clearly tells us what to think and what not to think.

According to Galatians 5:22-23, when you became a Christian, God imparted the fruit of the Holy Spirit into you and part of the fruit of the Spirit is self-control. No one has control over your mind and your thoughts but you. But if they do, it's because you allowed it.

How do we change our wants and desires into true hope? True hope comes from the same source as faith. You can't have one without the other. If you need a miracle, you have to see yourself in the state of living in the miracle. When it looks like all is lost, that's when you should quit looking. Take your eyes off the circumstances and put them on the Word of God. See yourself the way God sees you. Imagine yourself set free.

You must develop your hope and your faith so that you can imagine victory. Seeing it in the realm of the spirit is your first step in believing for it. If you cannot imagine it, that is your first clue that you must build up your faith.

Chapter 7

Faith Is Essential for Your Deliverance

Now faith is the substance of things hoped for, the evidence of things not seen.

Hebrews 11:1

Faith is essential in activating the Word of God. In these end times, there has been given a greater revelation of the importance and power of faith. Faith in its simplest form is just believing God, but in the realm of the spirit it is the substance that activates the power of God, which is His grace.

Faith Is a Tangible Substance in the Unseen Realm

Several years ago, I was reunited with one of my childhood friends. We had grown up together at Spring Valley Baptist

Church, but the years had not taken our friendship. He had recently purchased a nice house in the Kansas City area and even though the furniture had not been delivered yet, Loretta and I were invited to his house for an evening of fellowship and Bible study. There were only a few of us there, so we sat on the carpeted floor in his living room.

As we were reading scriptures, singing worship choruses, and praying, I looked across the room and saw an opening. It was about four feet tall in the shape of an oval mirror or window that looked very similar to the cutaway you might see in a video showing interpreters signing for the deaf. It was as though I was looking through a portal into another dimension. The lights were on, my eyes were open, and I clearly saw this. This was not a dream, but what some might call an open-eyed vision. I could tell that no one else in the room saw what I was seeing.

As I looked past the people across from me into an area that seemed to be a few feet behind them, I could see what looked like several long shards of crystal that were connected into a single unit that floated in the oval space. I didn't know exactly what I was seeing, but I was clearly seeing something quite astonishing! I said nothing to the others in the room, but kept it in my heart.

Several months later, I was the guest speaker at a local Baptist church. As I was preaching from the platform, I glanced at the back wall of the church and there I saw the exact same opening that I had seen before at the Bible study in Kansas City. In the opening were what appeared to be the exact same crystal shards connected in a unit floating within the oval space. Without missing a beat in my message, I continued to observe this opening for what seemed like several minutes before it was gone. Again, I did not reveal this to the congregation.

Later, during a quiet time with the Lord, I asked Him what it was that I had seen. Although it was not an audible voice, He clearly spoke to my heart and said, "You've seen into the spirit realm. The object you saw floating was the substance called faith." I felt as though He was telling me that He had allowed me to see into the realm of the spirit to see the substance of faith because the teaching of faith and its importance would be a major part of my life and calling.

From that day forward, faith has been more than a concept to me. It is not a metaphor, it is not an illusion, it is not a theory, but I know without a doubt it is a tangible substance in the realm of the invisible that activates the visible power of God in this realm.

Of course, Satan is a deceiver who wastes no time in developing a counterfeit to the plan of God. I think it's interesting that crystal is used by the enemy in the New Age cult.

What I saw looked like shards of crystal. In the Bible there are several verses that speak of things in heaven that look like crystal: a jasper stone (Revelation 21:11), a sea of glass (Revelation 4:6), and a pure river of water of life (Revelation 22:1), all appearing to look like crystal.

When you speak your confessions of hope and faith in this realm, you are actually building the substance in the spirit realm that will activate your deliverance. For this reason, it is extremely important not to allow faith and hope to become abstract ideas or concepts. The spirit of faith is living and tangible; it is the catalyst that activates your promise.

The Revelation of Truth

I have always believed that when working on an electrical appliance, the first thing to do is unplug it. That's just common sense. I believed that when working on an unplugged appliance, it would be impossible to get shocked or electrocuted. Right?

Years ago, I had a microwave that quit working. I based my faith on my belief that if I unplugged the microwave, I could remove the back panel to work on it and nothing could hurt me. So I unplugged it and removed the back panel to look inside. After all, this is the macho thing to do before you send it off to the repair shop! Most men don't want their wives to know they don't know how to fix something, so they always make a token attempt before sending it to someone who really knows what to do.

Inside I saw a lot of wires and components. It looked like the inside of an old-time pinball machine. I didn't know how to fix pinball machines either.

After looking inside long enough for my wife to think that I really knew what I was looking for, I decided everything looked okay. It was at that time I placed my right hand on the micro-wave and leaned against the refrigerator to think. All of a sudden, what felt like a million gigavolts of electricity shot through my body! I staggered back. I thought I was going to die. With one hand on my chest, for some strange reason I looked at my watch. I must have wanted to know the time that I was dying. My watch was a digital LED with red numbers, and it looked like it was speaking in tongues!

I don't know how many thousands of volts are stored in the capacitors within a microwave, but later I learned from an electrical engineer that even with the appliance unplugged, it stays fully charged. My watch died that day! I didn't die, but through this event I learned a great truth. Just because we believe something to be true does not make it true.

Regardless of how much we believe it is true, or how much we act like it is true, or regardless of how much we confess it, if it isn't true, it is false. And if we act on something that isn't true, it can mean death. My belief that I could not get shocked by an unplugged appliance was a partial truth. A partial truth has the appearance of truth but contains an untruth and that can be very deceiving. Only believing the whole truth will set us free. Only believing the complete truth will protect us from the destruction and possible death that comes from the deception of a partial truth.

Faith Never Fails

A few decades ago when the revelation of faith was first given to many great men and women of God, there were some Christians who only acted upon a partial truth so they did not receive results they expected. Critics quickly labeled their actions as "faith-failures." However, there is no such thing as a faith-failure. *Faith-failure* is an oxymoron because faith never fails.

So, what was the problem? Why did it appear that faith had failed? The answer is obvious. They did not have a true definition or understanding of faith. Only what is based on the truth will bring freedom.

The Bible tells us clearly the definition of faith. Faith is the substance of things hoped for and the evidence of things not seen (Hebrews 11:1). Let's break down this definition to examine it closely so that we can fully understand how to break free from despair and walk in hope.

Faith Is

Now faith is the substance of things hoped for, the evidence of things not seen.

Hebrews 11:1

First of all, **faith is**. The scripture does not say faith was or faith will be; it says faith is. While faith is a gift that grows and it can be small or great, this definition is referring to mature faith. Mature faith doesn't look backward by being linked to guilt of the past, nor does it look forward to the uncertainty of the future. Mature faith is established and built upon a foundation of God's Word that lives vibrantly in the present. Faith is.

Faith Is the Substance

Faith is **the substance**. There are two worlds: there is the original world known as the spirit world and the created world known as the physical world. While faith cannot be seen with our natural eyes, in the realm of the spirit, faith is a tangible substance. The substance of faith grows and becomes more powerful as our belief in the Word of God increases. Once the substance of faith has fully matured, it becomes the catalyst that activates the power of God's promise, which is His grace.

While we live in the physical realm, we reach into the realm of the spirit with our words of faith. The spoken belief in our heart apprehends the faith in the realm of the spirit and pulls it into the realm of the physical, activating God's promise that brings victory.

The Substance of Things Hoped For

Faith is the substance **of things hoped for**. Bible hope can be defined as the intense expectation that the promise of God will be fulfilled. While hope is not faith, hope is essential in attaining faith, for without hope in a promise from God, there is nothing to apply your faith to. While some have ridiculed hope, calling it unessential, in reality hope is extremely essential.

Hope is developed by hearing that deliverance is possible and promised by the Word of God. Hope brings the possibility of victory into one's heart where despair once resided. Hope is the distant flickering light in the dark that reveals the possibility that destruction is not imminent but that victory can be attained.

Although some ridicule hope, there are two things we must always remember. Paul said that we should hold fast the confession of our hope (Hebrews 10:23). In 1 Corinthians 13:13, we are told there are three things we are to abide or continue in: faith, hope, and love. While we are told that the greatest of these three is love, never forget that hope made it to the top three.

The Evidence of Things Not Seen

Faith is the substance of things hoped for and **the evidence of things not seen**. In a court of law, victory or defeat is based upon the evidence shown. The courtroom of God is in the spirit world but remember, the spirit world cannot be seen from the physical world unless supernaturally revealed by the Holy Spirit.

Even though the substance called faith that has been built by the revelation of the Word of God may not be visible in the physical realm, it becomes the evidence in the courtroom of heaven. Our faith becomes the proof our Advocate needs when presenting our case. The Judge is committed by the precedence of His own Word, so when the evidence of faith is presented, He must pronounce the verdict that He promised. The promise is then moved from the realm of the unseen into the realm of our physical existence. Healing, prosperity, and deliverance are the outcome of the trial because the Judge in heaven has proclaimed that He has been pleased by our faith.

Faith is believing that God has done what He said He would do, and believing it so much that everything we say and everything we do is based upon that belief. While hope is a good thing, we must always remember that hope looks forward to the promise of God while faith believes that the promise is here right now.

Someone might say, "But I don't see it. How can I say it's here if I don't see it?" Paul addressed this issue when he made the statement that we walk by faith and not by sight (2 Corinthians 5:7). In other words, we believe what God says in spite of what we may or may not see. In its simplest form, faith is believing God.

If a person just simply believes God, then faith will grow and become strong. With all the definitions that scholars have come up with through the years, by far the best definition of faith is the one given by God in His Word. Faith is the substance of things hoped for, the evidence of things not seen (Hebrews 11:1).

While this phrase ultimately defines faith, many times we still need greater understanding. Because of this, the following outline is to help you understand faith.

Seven Reasons Why We Need Faith

I truly believe that if you can grab hold of this, it will change your life. This is deliverance that can happen every single time. Here are seven basic reasons why faith is essential in living a life of victory.

Reason # 1 - Faith pleases God.

When you believe God, it pleases Him. Hebrews 11:6 says, "Without faith, it is impossible to please Him." The Spirit of God will move over the entire earth, over millions of people, looking for one person who will stand up and say, "I believe what You said" (Luke 18:8).

If not believing God is a sin (Romans 14:23), if believing God brings Him pleasure, and since He is the One with all the miracle power (Psalm 77:14), wouldn't it be good to please God? We please Him by believing Him. He is a rewarder of those who diligently seek Him by faith (Hebrews 11:6).

Reason #2 - We are saved by faith.

For by grace you have been saved through faith, and that not of yourselves; it is the gift of God.

Ephesians 2:8

Ephesians 2:8 says it clearly. If you think that everyone is saved because Jesus died for everybody, you are taking things out of context. Go back to John 3:16 that says "whosoever believes." It takes faith to get saved. He may have died for everybody, but the only people who receive eternal life are "whoever believes." Faith is required for salvation.

> If you confess with your mouth the Lord Jesus and believe in
> your heart that God has raised Him from the dead, you will
> be saved.
>
> Romans 10:9

Reason # 3 - We receive the Holy Spirit by faith.

Luke 11:13 says that the Father will give the Holy Spirit
to those who ask. But Galatians 3:2 explains that receiving the
Holy Spirit involves faith. We must apply this spiritual principle: for everything we desire to receive from God, we first must
believe enough to ask, but we must ask in faith.

> If you then, being evil, know how to give good gifts to your
> children, how much more will your heavenly Father give the
> Holy Spirit to those who ask Him!
>
> Luke 11:13

> This only I want to learn from you: Did you receive the Spirit
> by the works of the law, or by the hearing of faith?
>
> Galatians 3:2

Reason # 4 - Faith heals.

There are many examples in the Bible of Jesus proclaiming
that a person's faith had healed them. One that we discussed
earlier is the woman who experienced a severe health problem
for twelve years and who had spent all of her money on doctors
(Luke 8:43). Because of her physical condition, it was against the
law for her to be in public or to touch a man. The penalty was
death. But she had heard and believed and even told people that
if she could touch the hem of His garment, she would be healed.
She risked her life to get to Jesus, but when she touched Him,
she was healed.

Remember the powerful statement Jesus made concerning her healing. He said, "Daughter, your faith has made you well" (Luke 8:48). He publicly pronounced that her healing was a direct result of her faith.

Likewise James, the brother of Jesus, who later became the pastor of the church in Jerusalem, made the following statement in his letter to the church: "And the prayer of faith will save the sick, and the Lord will raise him up" (James 5:15).

Jesus healed the sick and the sick were healed in the church under the New Covenant, but we must remember that in every instance, faith was the key.

Reason #5 - Faith moves our prayers.

We are clearly told that when we pray, we must pray in faith. Praying in faith uses our authority and moves mountains. Doubt and unbelief moves nothing.

> But let him ask in faith, with no doubting, for he who doubts is like a wave of the sea driven and tossed by the wind. For let not that man suppose that he will receive anything from the Lord.
>
> James 1:6-7

Reason #6 - Anything not of faith is sin.

Romans 14:23 says, "But he who doubts is condemned if he eats, because he does not eat from faith; for whatever is not from faith is sin." That's a hidden nugget right there: if it's not faith, it's sin. Here Paul was writing a letter to the Christians who were living in Rome and were under the New Covenant. He told them that anything not of faith is sin. What is "not of faith?" It is when you don't believe what God said. If God says something and you believe Him, that's faith. Faith is believing God. Not believing God is not faith, but rather unbelief or doubt, and that is sin.

For example, we know that God wants us well and has given us instructions for healing in James chapter 5. Jesus said that He did not do anything unless the Father told Him to do it, and He went about in every town and village healing all who were sick (Matthew 9:35). So obviously, God must have told Him to do that. God himself proclaimed in Psalms 103:3 that He was the Lord our God who heals us.

So, anytime we doubt His desire to heal us, we do not believe what He told us. When we don't believe what He has told us, we are not in faith. Once again, anything not of faith is sin.

If you live your entire life not believing that God heals (Psalm 103:3), not believing that God delivers (Psalm 50:15), not believing that God gave you authority (Luke 10:19), not believing that God will protect you from the enemy (2 Thessalonians 3:3), or not believing that God wants you to prosper (Psalm 35:27), you are living outside the realm of faith, and God's Word says this is sin.

If you want to get delivered, believe what God is telling you. Don't second guess Him!

Reason #7 - Our faith overcomes the world.

For whatever is born of God overcomes the world. And this is the victory that has overcome the world—our faith.

1 John 5:4

In the natural world in which we live, there have been countless books written about how to overcome depression. But ultimately there is only one place where deliverance can be found and only one substance that produces freedom and victory. The Word of God is the source of our deliverance and the substance of faith is what activates it.

The Catalyst

Many years ago, my family owned a boat factory in Kansas. The boats were made out of fiberglass, which is a liquid. When that liquid fiberglass is poured into a boat mold, it becomes a boat. If it is poured into a counter top mold, it becomes a counter top for your bathroom. All kinds of things can be made out of fiberglass, because it is a liquid that can become whatever the mold designates it to be.

However, for it to become the finished product, the catalyst (which is called hardener) must be added to it. When the hardener is added to the fiberglass, it permanently becomes whatever it is designated to be. But it won't be anything except liquid until the catalyst is added.

Faith is the catalyst in the unseen spiritual realm. Jesus said in Acts 1:8, "You shall receive power when the Holy Spirit has come upon you." That power is to heal, that power is to deliver, that power is to restore, that power is to forgive, that power is for all kinds of things. Your speaking will move the mountains, split the water, and do whatever needs to be done supernaturally when you add the catalyst of faith.

The grace of God is the power of God working in you. The grace for your financial deliverance is available and activated when you add the catalyst of faith.

The Bible says if you believe that Jesus Christ is the Son of God, believe in your heart that God raised Him from the dead and confess it, you are saved (Romans 10:9). What is believing in the heart? It's the catalyst. "For God so loved the world that He sent His only begotten Son, that whosoever believes in Him..." (John 3:16). That's the catalyst: "Whoever believes in Him" – not everybody, but whoever believes! The grace is there for everyone to be saved, but the only ones who get saved are the ones who add the catalyst to it. "For by grace you are saved through faith" (Ephesians 2:8).

Make it personal: "This is the victory that has caused me to overcome in my life - my faith" (1 John 5:4). All seven of these reasons come down to one thing: faith is the substance of things hoped for and the evidence of things not seen. You don't have to see it, but you have to believe it, because you walk by faith, not by sight (2 Corinthians 5:7).

The Four Building Blocks of Faith

Every mechanical device has components that must fit together and work together in order to do the task it was created to do. While the number of components may vary, there is one factor that is consistent. Each component must work as designed to coordinate with the other components for the device to work properly. From a complicated item, like a space station, to a simple device, like the stapler sitting on your desk, every object, regardless of its complexity, can malfunction if one part is missing or doesn't function correctly.

So it is with faith. Faith has four basic components as described in the Word with each being essential for faith to function. I call them the four building blocks of faith.

I recognize that most of the concepts in the Four Building Blocks of Faith have at least been mentioned earlier, but because they are such important concepts, they are discussed here again so that all of the information is together in a concise teaching format on faith.

Building Block #1 -
You must know that God cannot lie.

During the early years of my ministry, I attended a meeting of 300 Christian leaders who gathered from around the world. I was young and not well-known, but the meeting was at a convention center near my ministry. Because of my friendship with a few ministers who were attending, I was invited even though this meeting was not advertised or open to the public. The purpose was to share the Word of God on an apostolic level. I was greatly honored to even be in the room with these great men of God.

Early one day before the morning meeting, I got on the elevator and to my amazement one of my great heroes of the faith, Dr. T.L. Osborn, was the only person in the elevator. He was the featured speaker for the morning session as well as the evening session. Either the elevator quit working or time was suspended, because in that short God-moment in the elevator, Dr. Osborn shared with me what God had put on his heart. He imparted to me two truths that changed my life and ministry forever.

He told me the title of his morning message was *God Cannot Lie,* and the text for this message was Titus 1:2 and Hebrews 6:18. Then he shared with me his title for the evening message. It was entitled *Satan is a Liar.* His text for that message was going to be John 8:44 where Jesus stated clearly that Satan was a liar and there was no truth in him.

During this time, digital media was not yet available so everything was recorded on reel-to-reel or cassette tapes. I took those two sermons and listened to them over and over again.

That was when I began to realize that the teaching that God cannot lie is a foundational truth that is required for faith. Without this understanding, faith can never be attained.

If it is possible that one word spoken from the mouth of God could be untrue, then every word spoken by Him would be in question. In other words, to walk in the power of God with faith, you must believe unconditionally that every word of God is true and not up for debate or to be questioned, but it must be accepted immediately and assuredly. This is the first building block of faith.

Building Block # 2 - You must know the Word of God.

Once you have established in your heart the unwavering reality that you do believe God's Word, the next step is to know what God says. There are those who say they believe God and believe what He has said in His Word, but they have not actually read the Holy Bible in its entirety, not even once. Sadly, many church-attending Christians only have a few scriptures they live by and sometimes these are even taken out of context. The bottom line is this: if you are committed to believing what someone says, you must know what that someone said.

In the book of Hosea, God said that His people are destroyed for a lack of knowledge (Hosea 4:6). This knowledge is not referring to world events or to secular scholastic studies, but to the knowledge of His Word. Paul the apostle encouraged the church to study in order to show themselves approved (2 Timothy 2:15). God's Word is not to be a casual document glanced over or only understood by reading a paraphrased review, but God's Word should be meditated on so the Holy Spirit can reveal to you the depth of the heart of God.

Romans 10:17 says that faith comes by hearing and hearing by the Word of God. This one passage is the only passage in the entire Bible that clearly tells us how faith comes. Faith does not come by hearing the news. Faith does not come from a testimony. Testimonies can bring encouragement and be uplifting, but faith only comes when the Word of God is revealed in the heart. Someone may say, "But I've heard testimonies that build my faith." This is possible, but only when the testimony contains the Word of God, because it is the Word of God within the testimony that builds faith. The testimony itself only brings encouragement. How do I know this? Because I believe the Word, and the Word says faith comes by hearing and hearing by the Word of God.

Building Block #3 - You must speak His Word.

When God created man, He created man in His own likeness and His own image. *Image* has to do with appearance, while *likeness* refers to resemblance of action. In other words, God created mankind to look like and act like Him. While we are not created to be God, as His children we are told to imitate Him (Ephesians 5:1). God created the universe by speaking it into existence. God said, "Let there be light," (Genesis 1:3) and there was light.

The Hebrew word for *let there be light* is *or* which is literally rendered *light be* or *light is*. When God stepped into the darkness, He proclaimed that the light was when it wasn't. He proclaimed what He wanted to exist as though it did exist. By doing this, what wasn't visible became visible, and there was light. The Bible says it this way: "He calls those things that do not exist as though they did" (Romans 4:17). He knew that when He spoke, He would have whatever He said. God is a faith God. Likewise, we are to be faith people who call things that do not exist as though they did.

When Jesus was talking to His disciples in Mark 11:22, He told them to have faith in God, or we could say to have the God-kind of faith. Then He went on to tell them that if they would speak to the mountain and believe in their heart that what they said would come to pass, they would have whatever they said.

> For assuredly, I say to you, whoever says to this mountain, 'Be removed and be cast into the sea,' and does not doubt in his heart, but believes that those things he says will be done, he will have whatever he says.
>
> Mark 11:23

In my life I've heard hundreds of sermons on this passage, and most theologians have taught that faith is believing that when you speak to the mountain, the mountain will be moved. But look closely at what Jesus actually said. He said, "If you speak to the mountain and believe that the words **you say** will come to pass, then you will have **whatever you say**." The mountain being moved into the sea is the result of believing in the power of your words spoken in faith.

Your words enter the spirit realm. When the Hebrews were in the wilderness, they grumbled about Moses while they were in their tents. The Bible says that their words entered God's presence and made Him angry (Deuteronomy 1:34).

Most Christians do not realize the power of the words they speak, but even though the power may be unrecognized, it is still there. That's why Jesus cautioned the Pharisees to be watchful of every word they spoke, whether it was intentional or not and whether they gave it any meaning or not. He called those "idle words" and said that men would have to give account for every word in the day of judgment. He also said they would be justified or condemned by those very words (Matthew 12:36-37).

Faith knows and believes God's Word so strongly that everything that is spoken aligns itself with the belief in the heart. When we know and believe that God's Word is true, then from our heart we speak as though it is already accomplished, even though we may not see the full manifestation with our eyes. Again, if God's Word says one thing and we see something else, our words must align with God's promise instead of with the circumstances.

Proverbs 6:2 says that we are snared by the words of our mouth. Too often, Christians are tempted to speak what they see. When they see a circumstance that looks bad or when they hear a bad report, they casually speak what they've seen or repeat what they've heard. Sadly, too many Christians have become so dulled by the world that the promises of God seem like wishful thinking rather than an established truth.

I've often heard the phrase, "I just speak it the way I see it." While that may sound logical and like you're speaking truth, in reality, it's only the facts of the circumstance being spoken. The truth of God, spoken by faith, can change the circumstances and make the visible facts irrelevant.

Imagine if God had used this line of thinking when He stepped into the darkness. Instead of saying, "Let there be light," He would have said, "Oh my goodness, it's dark," and the result would have been darkness instead of light. God received what He spoke because He calls things that be not as though they were (Romans 4:17 KJV). We as His children created in His image and likeness are to imitate Him (Ephesians 5:1). So we must call things that be not as though they are, also.

Through the years, I have had people approach me to tell me that while they were standing in faith, they were calling those things that be not as though they were. I remember asking a man, "If you're calling those things that be not as though they are, then what is your confession?" This man, who had sickness in his body, responded, "My confession is, 'I am not sick.'" He was shocked when I told him his so-called faith confession was not a confession of faith, but rather a statement of denial.

While he thought he was calling the thing that was not as though it was, in reality he was calling the thing that was as though it was not. Instead of proclaiming that he was healed (faith), he was doing exactly the opposite by saying he was not sick (denial).

We are to call into existence the promise we have been given which is faith. Our proclamation that the attack has not come or that we do not see a problem is denial. This one thing alone is a very subtle attempt by the enemy to confuse our speech to make people believe they are confessing the promise, when they actually are not. *Denying the problem is not the same as confessing the promise.*

Jesus clearly told us to speak to the mountain and believe in our heart. If you see a mountain in your path, don't stand there and say, "There is no mountain in my path!" That line of thinking will hinder you from speaking to the mountain and taking the authority that you have been given. After all, how can you speak to a mountain that you are confessing isn't there?

Building Block #4 - You must act on His Word.

In his letter to the church, James, the brother of Jesus, gave instructions on how faith works. He told them very clearly that faith without works is dead (James 2:26). In other words, faith must be living and active. Throughout my life, I have encountered many people who say one thing but do something else. In order for faith to function, our actions must reflect the belief in our heart and our confessions.

The work of faith is revealed in our daily lives through the fruit of the Spirit. If we truly believe the Word of God, our lives will be overflowing with love, joy, peace, longsuffering, kindness, goodness, faithfulness, gentleness, and self-control (Galatians 5:22-23). When our relationships with our friends, family, and neighbors are founded on the fruit of the Spirit, then the work of faith is fully mature in our lives. As a result, we will find joy in giving as well as thinking of others more highly than ourselves. The ultimate work of faith is the manifestation of godly love in our lives.

Your Hope Is Your Rope

When you feel like you're falling with no way out of your situation, you desperately look for something to hold onto, something you can grasp that will sustain you and keep you from destruction until you can find firm footing on which to stand.

Your hope is the rope that you cling to when you are falling. Your hope appears as you believe in the promise that God has given you. As you're holding onto the rope of hope, dangling above the destruction, you must continue to believe and speak God's promise. As you do, building blocks of faith are being put together inches below your feet.

As you continue without wavering in your belief and confession while holding onto your rope (hope), the foundation continues to be built. At some point the building blocks of faith will touch your feet and you will be able to walk in the deliverance God has provided.

First comes knowing without seeing, but as you continue to hold onto your hope, it develops into knowing and seeing. Faith is the substance you experience by walking on what in the beginning you couldn't see, because it wasn't there. But through your confession of hope, it becomes the visible substance of your deliverance.

Positive Thinking vs. Faith

Without faith it is impossible to please God. Faith believes that God has fulfilled His promises to us, and we acknowledge that belief through our confessions and actions. While faith confessions are always positive because they reflect the goodness of God in our lives, to those not understanding faith, it may appear that we are living in a fantasy world where we will never acknowledge anything wrong in our lives. Although it may appear this way to people who do not understand faith, we know that God is a good God (James 1:17), and we know that He is the one who brings healing to our lives (Psalm 103:3). We know God is not evil, and He does not teach us through pain and suffering (trials).

So, when someone hears a believer speaking a promise from God, it might sound like they are caught up in positive thinking instead of faith. But for the person who believes the Word of God in their heart, nothing could be further from the truth. Of course, positive thinking is always better than negative thinking, but the truth is this: the positive Word of God settles in our heart by way of the continual washing of our mind with the Word of God. As we study and meditate on God's Word, the seed (the

Word of God) settles into our heart (the field) where faith is established. Once faith is established, our words will change to show a harvest of truth that comes from our mouth. Jesus put it this way. He said, "Out of the abundance of the heart the mouth speaks" (Matthew 12:34).

Positive Thinking

While positive thinking doesn't compare to the faith that God's Word brings, it is still better than doubt and unbelief. There are natural results that come from positive thinking. The salesman that has faith in himself and his product will have much more success than a salesman who does not. However, never forget that faith in God is much more powerful than faith in yourself.

I once attended a sales seminar led by a presenter who was known by many as the "world's greatest salesman." Books were written about his success and, at the time of the seminar, he was appearing as a guest on several network talk shows. When asked about the key to his success as a salesman, his response was, "You must have faith."

This man was not known for his Christian faith, but only well known for his sales ability. He moved up in his company regardless of the position he was placed in, until eventually he became the national vice-president in charge of sales, even though he did not have any formal marketing training nor a degree in business management.

Although everyone who worked for him had formal sales training, he outsold them all and became a sales trainer. In his training sessions, he taught that the number one factor in sales is faith. He said you must believe that your product is the best, and you must believe that it works the way it is supposed to work. But you must also believe that when this product is presented properly, it will be purchased. He said when you sell by faith, there is a confidence that is transmitted which can be seen by the purchaser. This confidence assures, calms, and encourages.

Early in his career he was hired by a company even though many others who had applied had better resumès. When the person in charge of human resources was asked why he hired him, he smiled and said, "I don't know. He just talked me into it so I thought if he can do that, he must be a good salesman. He had faith in himself."

Although positive thinking is powerful, it doesn't compare to the faith that is produced when we believe the Word of God. Not only do the natural principles of confidence and trust apply, but the staggering, unmeasurable power of God is unleashed when true faith in God's Word is spoken.

What You Say Is What You Get

As those around us hear the positive promises of God coming from our mouths, they may think it's only the result of positive thinking training. But for the Christian who has been sowing the Word in his or her heart, it is the harvest of faith.

Someone may say, "How can you proclaim that God is fulfilling your dream? How can you claim that you have hope in His promise when everything around you looks like your dream is dead and you have no hope?" "After all," they may say, "we know it is true in life that what you see is what you get." The reality is, that statement is not true. For the believer who is walking in faith, instead of what you *see* is what you get, the truth is, what you *say* is what you get.

Entering His Rest

In the early years of my ministry as the pastor of a Southern Baptist church, one of the things I believed and taught my congregation was this: the Word of God always works and nothing can keep His Word from working. Then one day while reading my Bible, I encountered a verse that shook my core belief. This verse told of two groups of people who heard the Word and the Word they both heard was the same gospel. But the Word the first group heard was totally unprofitable to them simply because it was not mixed with faith in their hearts. How could this be? Are His promises conditional? Is faith the catalyst that activates the promises? According to the Bible, the answer is yes!

> For indeed the gospel was preached to us as well as to them; but the word which they heard did not profit them, not being mixed with faith in those who heard it.
>
> Hebrews 4:2

This passage reveals that this same gospel was preached to two groups of people. The first group who heard the gospel were the Hebrews who were taken out of Egypt. The good news of deliverance was preached to them. All they had to do was believe God, cross the Jordan, and enter into Canaan, the land flowing with milk and honey. It was the place of rest that God had chosen for His people. God's plan was to deliver the land to them. All they had to do was put their faith in Him and the land would be theirs. They rejected His promise, and as a result, they wandered in the wilderness for forty years.

Likewise, the gospel, the good news of deliverance, was preached to us. As New Covenant people, Jesus has paid the price in full for us to enter into a place of victory. We have been given promises of life, health, healing, and prosperity. Like the Hebrews of old, we also have a choice. Do we remain in bondage or do we accept His promise and enter into His rest?

Again, Hebrews 4:2 reminds us that although the Word was preached to the Hebrews, it did not profit them because it was not mixed with faith in their hearts. They did not believe the promise of God, therefore they did not receive the promise of God. Every Israelite who was above the age of twenty (with the exception of Joshua and Caleb) died before the Hebrews entered the promised land. Believing in and accepting His promise by faith brings blessings. Not believing in and rejecting His promises keeps us from receiving His blessings.

Once Jesus' disciples asked Him what the work was that they were to do. His response was, "To believe in Him" (John 6:28-29). Jesus did all the work and everything was completed when He said on the cross, "It is finished" (John 19:30). Now we must rest in what He has completed. Every day born-again believers are standing at the Jordan, making the decision: Do I believe God, cross over, and enter into His rest today? Or do I reject His promises, pick up the cares of the world, and begin my day with stress, tension, apprehension, and worry?

His rest is vital to the Christian lifestyle. As a born-again believer, this must be a daily walk with a conscious effort being made at the beginning of each day. Today I will enter into His rest. Today I believe His Word. Today I am healed. Today I am prosperous. Today I have the joy of the Lord. Today I will be led by His Spirit.

All of this cannot be done from a place of frustration, but rather it must come from the foundation of rest. Before your feet hit the floor in the morning, enter into His rest.

Keep Your Faith Tank Full

As a teenager riding around in my 1960 Pontiac Bonneville, a two-door coupe with long, Cadillac tail lights, I felt cool! The car's white-rolled, pleated-leather interior and blue lights in my fender wells were something to behold. The metallic, midnight-blue, special paint job added to this classic show car. The only problem was, I kept running out of gas. With teenagers, some things seem to never change!

My dad was a brilliant businessman and even though I didn't always listen to his advice, he taught me one thing that has been proven true throughout the years. He said, "It's just as easy to keep your gas tank between three-quarters and full as it is to keep it between one-quarter and empty." Unfortunately, many who attempt to run off the top quarter of the tank instead of the bottom quarter of the tank see everything below three-quarters as a safety net, which is why they also postpone getting fuel, and eventually run out anyway.

In life, concerning our faith, we should have the mentality of keeping the tank full and when we see it get down to three-quarters full, fill it up again. In other words, we should continually keep our faith tank full by daily filling ourselves with the Word. The Bible is your gas station for faith and hope. If you only fill your tank on Sunday, you may be nearing empty by Thursday. You cannot afford to take a vacation from maintaining your faith. It must be a lifestyle, not an event. Faith comes by hearing and hearing. Faith does not come by having heard. It must be continuous.

Chapter 8

Healthy Relationships

There are three relationships that must be healthy in your life in order for you to have the fullness of hope promised in God's Word. God has promised that we have hope for our future, but through the sum of the Scriptures we find that this hope is influenced by the health of these relationships: 1) your relationship with God; 2) your relationship with yourself; and 3) your relationship with others. As these relationships become balanced and in line with the Word, spiritually and physically, you will be able to step into the fullness of the plan and destiny that God has for you.

1. Your Relationship with God

> God is Spirit, and those who worship Him must worship in spirit and truth.
>
> **John 4:24**

Your relationship with God is unlike any other relationship you have on earth. Why? Because earthly relationships are based on physical and emotional circumstances that can be seen and felt. However, God is spirit, and He exists in the realm of the unseen.

As we said earlier, man was created as a three-part being in the likeness and image of God. God is Father, Son, and Holy Spirit. Likewise man is spirit, soul, and body. Because God is spirit and those who worship Him must worship Him in spirit and in truth, our connection and communication with God must be on a spiritual level. To worship, to pray, to make a request, or to give thanks are all communication with Father God.

Any relationship that is true must be based on honesty and never be deceptive or manipulative. Any deceptive communication with God is futile as He knows your heart better than you do. He knows what you need even before you speak it (Matthew 6:8). Remember, even though you have a free will and can speak from your head or your heart, God knows in advance what you will say and the motive behind it. A relationship with God is developed through honesty and obedience to the leading of His Spirit.

First John 5:14 says that we can have confidence when we talk with Him. We know if we simply stay within His will that He hears us. The next verse tells us that He grants our requests when we stay within His will in our communications and requests. Even Jesus, on the evening before He was crucified, expressed to the Father in prayer that He did not want to be nailed on the cross if there was any other way to redeem mankind. But then in submission, He made a powerful statement when He said, "Nevertheless not My will, but Yours, be done" (Luke 22:42).

In communicating and developing a relationship with God, we must never forget that the kingdom of heaven has a King and the King is God the Father. In a kingdom, the king rules and his will is the law of the land. To develop a relationship with the king, we must agree with the king. In the kingdom of God, this is easy because the King of the kingdom loves us so much that His desire is that we have eternal life, eternal prosperity, and eternal joy (John 10:10).

Father Knows Best

Sometimes children do not know what's good for them. They may be old enough to feed themselves, but they may think cake and ice cream should be eaten every meal. As a parent, we know that good nutrition is important, so a healthy meal is provided by the parents regardless of what the child desires. As the child matures with age and knowledge, they begin to understand that desserts may be pleasurable, but they cannot substitute for a healthy diet.

Likewise, as children of God, we must always realize that God knows more about what we need than we do. But we also must know that God is a good God who wants the best for us. His gifts are good and His gifts are designed for our benefit (James 1:17).

Our relationship with God also differs dramatically from our relationships with others concerning this one point. While our friends and relatives advise us to the best of their ability, treating us with varying degrees of kindness based upon emotions that are affected by the surroundings, God will always treat us justly and truthfully. In other words, while advice and motives of our earthly relationships must be judged by the Scriptures, God's Word does not need to be judged, but simply obeyed.

Our physical body needs food, exercise, and sleep at regular intervals to maintain our physical health. In the same way, our spirits need regular fellowship with God through worship, prayer, and time in His Word. In doing so, we keep clear revelation from Him in our hearts. Ultimately, our relationship with God will be the foundation for every other relationship in life, whether it be casual or intimate. Until this relationship is established and maintained, our surroundings will determine the joy and hope levels in our life. A person without a solid relationship with God will constantly be tossed back and forth like a wave of the sea and will be unstable in all his ways (James 1:6-8).

Getting Help from God

But seek first the kingdom of God and His righteousness, and all these things shall be added to you.

Matthew 6:33

Once I was contacted by a man who attended several of my meetings over the years. He sounded desperate for counsel, so we set a time to meet. Upon arriving at my office, we exchanged greetings and sat down to talk. Before I could say anything, he started explaining in great detail all of the complexities of his situation. Without stopping for any input from me, he continued to tell me of all the things he had thought of and done to remedy his problem.

Without taking a breath, he re-stated the severity of his problem and his frustration that nothing he had done had really helped. He said he knew he was losing hope because he had tried everything. The only thing left to do was pray. When everything else had failed, he finally turned to God. While it is good that he eventually thought about God, God should not have been his last resort.

I knew this man. He was a Christian, but like so many, he lived his life trying to accomplish his goals and solve his own problems. While it is true that God gives us wisdom for our journey through life on earth, He should not be relegated to the back seat while we try to figure out where we are going.

Being a pilot, I have seen plaques and stickers to put in the cockpit that say, "God is my co-pilot." While it's good to acknowledge that God is in the plane, wouldn't it be better to make Him the pilot? Making Him the Captain will save a lot of time and eliminate having to correct the course. When He's the captain who sets the course and we respond by following, the trip becomes stress free and enjoyable.

So, here's the point. When problems in life become unbearable and hope begins to fade, ask yourself this question: "Who is in the captain's seat?" If it's you, get up and move aside. Let God be your guide. Do it now! Don't wait until your plane is in trouble.

Your plane may be nosediving toward the ground and a crash may look imminent, but when you need a miracle, God has one for you. Once God miraculously delivers you out of your disaster, make sure you put Him in the captain's seat. Don't wait until a disaster to change places with Him.

In other words, maintain your hope by being proactive with it rather than constantly being in recovery mode. God's Word promises us health and healing. Healing is good, but if we continually walk in health, healing won't be necessary.

How Does God Help Us?

Most people, even Christians, don't realize that there is a parallel world with daily functions taking place. In this parallel world, there are ministering spirits who are looking into this world and watching us. Their sole purpose is to help us get past impossible problems and circumstances in life.

> **Are they not all ministering spirits sent forth to minister for those who will inherit salvation?**
>
> **Hebrews 1:14**

God's ministering spirits are called angels. They were created by God with a purpose. Man was not created for angels, but angels were created for man. Jesus did not die for angels. He died for man.

You can have hope knowing there are actual beings in existence who are watching you twenty-four hours a day with their purpose being to assist you when you need help.

> **For He shall give His angels charge over you, to keep you in all your ways.**
>
> **Psalm 91:11**

These unseen spirits in this parallel world do their work based upon the commands given by the person they are observing and wanting to assist. Unfortunately, because angels are unseen and the human mind tries to reason that they are just fantasy, many Christians don't activate them with commands from the Word of God, so problems tend to go unsolved. Many tragedies in life could have been averted if the knowledge and understanding of how to apply this assistance was understood. If you don't believe that something exists, or if you relegate it to fiction, in times of crisis you will instinctively ignore this powerful assistance provided by God.

Remember, Jesus told His disciples that they could move mountains when they spoke if they believed in their heart that the words they said would come to pass (Mark 11:23). How do you think the mountain actually gets moved? Does Jesus get up from the right hand of God, come to earth and move the mountain Himself? Does God stand up from His throne and come to earth to move the mountain? Or is it the Holy Spirit who lives inside of you? Does He move the mountain? No. It's the ministering angels, the ones who minister for those who will inherit salvation. They are the ones who actually move the mountain.

All through the Bible we see that angels move back and forth from the realm of the unseen into the realm of the seen (Genesis 28:12). The commands they are given are transmitted to them in the spirit realm and then carried out in this world.

Moving Mountains

Many times in the Bible when the term *mountain* is used, it is not referring to a physical mountain on earth, but a kingdom. For example, sometimes the mountain of God is referring to the kingdom of God. Likewise, the mountain that is blocking your path is the kingdom of darkness so you need this mountain moved to continue on the path to victory.

The Bible tells us in Psalm 103:20 that angels obey the voice of God's Word. For us, God's Word is recorded in the Holy Scriptures, but to put voice to His Word, we must speak those scriptures. So the key in having the angels move the mountain is to find a place in the Word where God promised your deliverance, then put voice to His Word.

> Bless the Lord, you His angels, who excel in strength, who do His word, heeding the voice of His word.
>
> Psalm 103:20

God has provided angels to do the work of moving the mountain out of your path. That is His will. But the angels only do the work for those who believe and confess the promise of God. While we do not place our faith in angels or worship them, the Bible tells us they are empowered to implement His promise when they hear the voice of His Word come from our mouths. The angels don't speak it, they implement it. You are the voice. At that point the scripture that says, "Angels are ministering spirits who minister for those who inherit salvation" (Hebrews 1:14), becomes fulfilled. That's talking about the Church. That's us!

How Do You Send Your Angels?

So, let's get down to the basic reality of this. How do we send our angels to move the mountain? As a Christian, you must know in your heart that God's Word is truth, that His promises to you are true, and that you speaking His promises activates the angels of God to fulfill them. Even if you do not see the finished results immediately, you continue to believe and speak the promise. You never give up on the promise, and you never quit believing that its manifestation is imminent. You stay steadfast in your confession of hope (Hebrews 10:23). The bottom line is this: you speak the Word of God by faith and the angels will bring it to pass.

Always remember this: Jesus is not an angel. He never has been one and He will never be one. Angels were created by God, the Creator. Likewise, you are not an angel and will never become one. Angels are created spirits who were created for the purpose of carrying out the spoken Word of God. You are the voice of His Word. When you speak, your words either bind your angels or release them to do the Word. By your own words you are helped or left without help. Your life and your death are in the power of your tongue (Proverbs 18:21).

The writer of Hebrews reminded the young Christians in the New Testament that when they encounter a stranger, they should treat him with hospitality because of the possibility that a stranger might actually be an angel (Hebrews 13:2).

So the next time you need a mountain moved—whether it be a mountain of debt, sickness, pain, or just an obstacle that's in the way—find the scripture that promises what you need done and send your angels to perform it by speaking the voice of His Word.

2. Your Relationship with Yourself

The way you see yourself and the way you feel about yourself is the pivotal relationship in your life. What I mean by this is even though your relationship with God may be in a good place, you will never develop wholesome relationships with others until you see yourself properly. In order to have the hopes and dreams of your life fulfilled, you must not only know whose you are, but also who you are. You must love yourself. The atmosphere that surrounds you will never be quite right until this is accomplished.

> **For all the law is fulfilled in one word, even in this: "You shall love your neighbor as yourself."**
>
> **Galatians 5:14**

From the time that Cain killed his brother Abel until now, conflict between family and friends has not ceased. As a pastor, I have noticed that throughout the decades of ministry this seems to be an issue that is consistent. The enemy has found this conflict as a weak place in the flesh of man that he can attack, which he does relentlessly.

In times of counsel, I tell people the same thing that Jesus told those He was teaching: we must forgive and do good to those who spitefully use us and hurt us (Matthew 5:44). Sometimes I've noticed that I don't see joy on the faces of those I am counseling. Why? It's usually because they are harboring unforgiveness and are waiting for a time when they can retaliate or get revenge. Quite obviously, they don't love the person with whom they are having the issue.

This is the root cause of low self-esteem and lack of self-respect. Without knowing it, many people are putting into practice a spiritual principle that hinders the blessings of God in their lives. The ultimate reason that people have problems forgiving and loving others is that they haven't forgiven and loved themselves. Jesus said, "Love your neighbor as yourself" (Mark 12:31). Some people hate their neighbors because they secretly hate themselves.

In order to have complete freshness and freedom in your life, you must not only have your relationship with God and others in balance spiritually and emotionally, but you must also have a good relationship with yourself. You must see yourself as God sees you, neither in arrogance nor in a prideful way, but in the knowledge that God loved you so much that while you were yet in sin, He sent His Son to die for you (Romans 5:8). His plan for you is a life filled with the goodness of His glory, not only in the future, but in the here and now. When you can love yourself with godly love and receive His blessings, you will be able to love and bless others. This sets the stage for your freedom.

Forgiveness Brings Deliverance

Several years ago a lady visited our church, and I noticed when I first met her that she seemed very sad. Although she was not rude, she was not very friendly either. After a few months, she and her husband made our church their church home and one day in conversation she told me her story.

As a young girl she was very outgoing, but as she grew into her early teen years, one of her relatives began to sexually molest her. This put her into a place of darkness that had continued throughout her life. She eventually met the love of her life, got married and did her best to keep the shadow of her past behind her. Her husband and her family were her life.

Then one day tragedy struck. Her young granddaughter was brutally murdered, and the murderer was not found. As we sat while she shared this heartbreaking story, I could feel her pain. I gently told her that to be set free from this bondage of the past, she had no choice but to forgive.

First of all, she had to forgive her relative. When I told her that, she abruptly leaned forward with great sternness on her face, her teeth and fists clenched, and said boldly, "I can't forgive him! He owes me! That man owes me!"

When I asked her where he was now, she wrinkled her forehead and said, "He died about twenty years ago." I looked back at her with a very serious look and said, "Here's the plan. You tell me where he's buried, then we'll go buy a new shovel, go to the cemetery, and dig him up. And I will personally let you be the first to rattle his bones and yell at him."

It was quiet. At first, she thought I was very serious, but then she began to laugh. Something had broken. The realization of the truth came to light. Yes, it was true the man owed her, but it was also true that he could never repay her. He could never give back her innocence that he had stolen. He could never give back her years of pain. It was impossible. The only thing she could do to gain her freedom was to forgive and laugh! In that moment, she forgave him, and the joy of the Lord poured out of her.

Then we moved to the subject of forgiving the man who killed her granddaughter. She said, "But what he did was wrong!" and she was right. The murderer destroyed a family and justice had not been served. I explained to her that forgiving him had nothing to do with him, and it did not mean that she condoned or accepted what he did. It was about her; it was about her heart. That day she said she would work on it. A couple of weeks later she met me in the atrium of the church, and with a smile on her face, said, "I don't like what he did, but I forgave him."

This lady became one of the happiest ladies in the entire congregation and was known for her laughter and joy! Her entire personality and attitude changed. People loved to be around her. This was one of the greatest deliverances from the bondage of darkness I have ever seen. As she loved herself, that love naturally poured out to her friends and family. By the way, the murderer was eventually caught.

3. Relationships with Others

Our relationship with God should be and can be a permanent, ongoing, intimate relationship, while many times our friendships with others are only for a season. Even family relationships change, and we must adjust to them throughout the changes of life. Education, employment, marriage, and retirement are things that can alter our relationships. Even the relationship of a parent to a child differs with the age of a child. Although the love and compassion seem to never change, a parent treats a five-year-old child much differently than a fifty-year-old child.

Because God never changes (Hebrews 13:8), our relationship with Him moves in a steady upward direction with ever increasing intensity. Loving God and submitting to Him is our only choice for victory. There is no other God, there is no other being, there is no other creation who can provide hope and victory like He has provided for us.

But although God doesn't change, people do. Our relationships with others many times seem to be in a constant state of flux. While relationships rise and fall because of the circumstances of life, there are some things that must be constant if we want to retain our joy as we fulfill the dream that God has given us.

This may seem to be overstated, but it is imperative that you choose your friends wisely. When you choose to keep friendships with people who you know are doing wrong, even though you have decided that you will not get involved with their wrongdoing, there can be painful, unintended consequences in your life.

Negative Influence of People

He who walks with wise men will be wise, but the companion of fools will be destroyed.

Proverbs 13:20

Many lives are enhanced or destroyed solely because of friendships or relationships with others. Through the years, I have known many intelligent, talented people with a vision for their life who failed because of the people they allowed into their life. A great truth comes from Proverbs 12:26 where the Bible states, "The righteous should choose his friends carefully, for the way of the wicked leads them astray."

Over the years, I have known many people who by their nature were very good, but their lives and their dreams were destroyed because of their associations. For example, I have an acquaintance who is a good man. He loves God and is fair in all his business dealings. But earlier in his life, he spent many years in prison for the armed robbery of a convenience store. Although he was found guilty, he actually wasn't the one who committed the crime.

My friend was driving with two of his friends when he noticed he needed fuel, so he pulled off at a convenience store. While he was filling his fuel tank, his two friends went inside. After refueling his car, he waited for his friends, and when they returned, they drove away. What he didn't know is that while his friends were inside the convenience store, they committed an armed robbery.

After they were apprehended by the police, the case went to trial. All three were on trial together and all three received the same prison sentence. Even though my friend didn't actually rob the store (in fact, he didn't even own a gun), he still received the same legal punishment. What was his downfall? It was his choice of companions.

This is an excellent example of how the people you associate with can destroy your life. However, there are subtle types of destruction that are not as dramatic as my friend going to prison, but they are potentially just as destructive and can cause a person to be a prisoner within their own mind or within their own house.

Going Along with a Bad Idea

When I was fourteen years old, most of my friends were a little older than I was. This didn't affect me very much until my older friends reached the age when they could drive. As soon as they started driving, they began to push the limit of what they could legally do. We were living in Raytown, Missouri at that time. My father worked the night shift at General Motors, and my only transportation to and from church youth group in the evenings was my friends who had recently obtained their drivers' licenses.

One evening as they picked me up for youth group, they informed me they had other plans. It was a warm summer night, and their plan was to drive through Swope Park and drink beer. I was shocked! No one in my family drank alcohol. As far as I knew, my friends had never drunk alcohol. Actually, that was true. This was their first night, but they had pulled out all the stops. They were going to be wild and crazy. I was in the back seat of their '58 Chevy, and there was no way I was going to tell my friends I wouldn't participate. Deep inside, I was worried that the police would have me in jail by morning.

As we rode around in the early summer night with all the windows down on our mint green two-door '58 Chevy Coupe, the thing I dreaded began to unfold. The boys in the front seat opened up the box that contained the six-pack of Pabst Blue Ribbon Beer.

Back in those days the beer cans were not like they are today. Today beer and soda cans have these handy little pop tops that even a very weak person could open, and the cans are made of very lightweight aluminum. But the cans that were being passed to the back seat of the '58 Chevy appeared to be made of cast iron! To open them, a device called a "church key" was used. It took great strength to pry the church key into the can and make an opening. Likewise, the church key had to be used on the other side of the can to equalize the pressure within the can. I'm sure this was an easy task for an experienced beer drinker of the day, but I had never seen a beer can that close, much less ever touched one. And there is a good possibility that no one else in the car had either.

The boys in the front seat were sixteen years old. The two of us in the back seat were fourteen. It was illegal for us to have beer in the car, much less drink it. But the two "older men" in the front seat were acting like they did it every day. As the other boys guzzled their beer, I'm sure it tasted horrible to them. But they were men! They drank their beer and threw the can out the window. As the can hit the pavement on that warm summer night, we could hear it go "tink, tink, tink" as it bounced toward the ditch.

What could I do? I knew my salvation did not depend on whether or not I drank the beer, but my church upbringing, and the fact that my mother told me Jesus was in the back seat with me, was bringing on a heavy burden of guilt. So I devised a plan. I stuck my tongue into the little hole made by the church key. I tilted the can up and brought it back down as I made satisfying sounds while saying, "Boy, that's good liquor!" After doing this three or four times, I figured it was about time for me to pretend my can was empty and throw it out the window like everybody else. But instead of my can going "tink, tink, tink," it just made one solid thunk. Although no one said a word, I knew they knew!

Looking back on the situation, I now realize that my friends were probably just as scared as I was that the police, our parents, or our pastor, the Reverend Joe C. Porter from Spring Valley Baptist Church, would discover our sin. That night there was no accident, no one got drunk, no one got caught, and we all kept our mouths shut.

The next Sunday at church the four of us kept silent. Our church had communion that Sunday, and I remember hoping that I didn't die. I remembered the scripture verse that said some people were sick and some had even died because they took the Lord's Supper in an unworthy manner (1 Corinthians 11:27-30). I had extensive prayer and closed my eyes as I took communion that Sunday.

But through the years, looking back on this experience, I realize that even good kids can be led astray by other good kids when they don't have wise counsel and guidance. Many lives have been destroyed because of a moment of weakness and submitting to the folly of a friend.

Everyone in the car had been raised in the church with Christian families. In fact, we were all very involved in the church. And each of us in that car that night was a member of the Spring Valley Baptist Bell Choir that performed at the Southern Baptist Convention. We were good kids with a bad idea.

Although we were good kids, none of us had the strength to say, "No! This is a bad idea. I'm not going to do it." If any one of the four would have said that, it probably would have never happened. You cannot surround yourself with friends who simply agree with everything you say because they want to be your friends. You must allow correction into your life and have relationships that allow others to speak truth without taking offense or breaking the relationship.

Ungodly Influence from Influential People

Blessed is the man who walks not in the counsel of the ungodly, nor stands in the path of sinners, nor sits in the seat of the scornful.

Psalm 1:1

One of the methods used to destroy hope and kill a dream is confusion. Confusion by its very nature is the lack of knowing the truth. When a person is confident in the knowledge that their future has been promised by God and their confidence is backed by a promise in the Word of God, there is no confusion. Truth always brings peace and joy from within. But when the truth is proclaimed and acted upon, the enemy will attempt to bring confusion and mistrust in the promise of God, and he often uses people to do this.

Once a young man, while attending a church retreat, was strongly led by the Spirit of God that he was to give his life to missions. He knew it was a call from God. He told me that when he made the decision, his heart was filled with joy. Even though he was young, he was not a complete novice. He had been on two overseas missions trips and had seen the work of missionaries firsthand. This was not a casual decision, but it was an answer to a call from God on his life. He could hardly wait to tell his family of the decision he had made.

The first to hear the news was his mother, but his mother was not a godly woman. Although she attended church from time to time, her lifestyle was not that of a Christian. In fact, at the time, she was having an affair with a married man while hiding it from her own husband. Upon hearing the news that her son was called to be a missionary, she abruptly said, "No! You can't do that. Missionaries do not make any money! You'll be poor all your life. I will not allow it."

Although the young man still believed he was called, and even though he was receiving counsel from a person who was living an ungodly life, out of respect for her as his mother, he yielded and gave up his dream for the time. He wanted to please God, and he wanted to please his mother. Although God had spoken to his heart, his mother continuously pressed her view upon her son. He became confused so he postponed his decision. Yet, by not making a decision, he had actually made a decision, so his dream to answer the call faded.

Positive Influence of People

One of the greatest desires in life is to be liked, loved, and to have a friend with whom you can share the deep secrets of your heart. Many times just by voicing the deep thoughts from within to someone who understands can clarify and sometimes even solve what seemed to be an unsolvable problem.

Several years ago, I was standing on a boat dock talking to a neighbor who was doing some repairs. Our small talk developed until at one point in our conversation, he opened up and told me he had always wanted to be a doctor. "My dream in my younger years was to be a surgeon," he said, "but because of the circumstances of life, I was unable to finish college and pursue my dream. To support my family I took odd jobs to pay the bills, but as the years passed, my dream died."

I asked him why his dream was dead. He replied, "Are you kidding? It would take seven more years of schooling for me to become a surgeon. Do you have any idea how old I would be in seven years if I went to school and got my degree?" Instinctively I responded, "Well, how old will you be in seven years if you don't go to school?"

I never will forget the look he gave me as the realization that his dream was still possible washed over him. That one conversation made him see that his dream was not dead. That very day he pursued going back to school to get his degree, and today he's a surgeon.

That day standing on the boat dock, looking out over the Lake of the Ozarks, a decision was made, a corner was turned, and a life was changed. Because of that moment of expressing the deep secrets of his heart, his life, the life of his wife and his children, and everything connected with him was changed. This man became a doctor because his God-given dream was brought back to life by words that were full of faith and hope.

Relationships to Avoid

A person walking in hope that is founded on a promise from God has confidence embedded deep in his or her heart that the promise will be fulfilled. Because of this, they do not need to exalt themselves through comparison with others, nor do they find it necessary to degrade or ridicule others to make themselves look better. Why? Again, because hope is established in the assurance that regardless of what goes on around you, and regardless of what has happened in your past, your future is secure and established by God's promise. It is in His promise that you have placed your hope. If someone criticizes you for having hope, avoid sharing your heart with them.

Avoid people who overanalyze and talk about your problem to the extent that it brings confusion. Confusion develops into disorder, and if the personalities are strong, strife may develop.

Good decisions are never made during times of strife. Hope is almost always lost in the presence of strife. When things look hopeless, one of the most critical decisions you can make is to remove yourself from confusion and strife. I have known people who could never come to a decision on any subject. They would discuss and analyze until all understanding of what was originally discussed was lost, and the result was confusion. Avoid these kinds of people.

> A perverse man sows strife, and a whisperer separates the best of friends.
>
> **Proverbs 16:28**

You should never share your dream with someone who sows strife or whispers stories about others. They will never give you godly counsel. They are just looking for information.

Likewise, there are those who actually look for people they can counsel because their sole purpose is to receive unknown information about dreams and desires so they can repeat it to others. In doing so, it makes them feel important to have knowledge that no one else has. In other words, their purpose in counseling you is to help them, not you. It is to make themselves feel important. They could care less about your dreams or your hope for the future. Avoid sharing your heart with these people.

> He who covers a transgression seeks love, but he who repeats a matter separates friends.
>
> **Proverbs 17:9**

While we are not supposed to judge or be critical of other people, we must still examine and evaluate the value of their friendships. Just because you determine a specific person should not be in your inner circle of friends because of their negative nature, it does not mean that you are condemning them. But you must distance yourself from those who speak anti-faith, and you do this through examination and evaluation of their friendship.

Guidelines in Seeking Advice

During the early years of my ministry, I worked for a short time in Kansas City as a marriage counselor. Actually, I only worked there one day. My office was in downtown Kansas City on the third floor of an office building that had not been remodeled since the 1930s. It reminded me of an office that a detective would have had in an old crime movie. The lighting was poor, the desk was old, and I was young without much experience. As I sat behind the desk early that morning wearing my white shirt and narrow black tie, I awaited my first counseling session. I looked like a NASA scientist working on the Apollo moon project with my pocket protector and my old rotary phone sitting on my desk.

Finally, the phone rang and a distraught woman was on the line. I said, "Family Aid Marriage Counseling. How may I help you?" Immediately, without even telling me her name, she said, "What do I do with a husband who won't stay at home and likes a lot of other women?" Before I could utter a word, she started telling me her story. She was very upset and very animated. My young ears heard things that I didn't even know happened in this world! I was shocked at what her husband had been doing. The more she talked, the more I knew I had no answers for her. I may have had some theological training at college, but I wasn't prepared for this! I told the other counselor, who was also a theological student, that I quit. I put my pocket protector on the desk, along with my key, and I left that day.

I'm sure the lady who called me thought she was calling a seasoned professional who could solve all her problems if she would just lay them at my feet. Little did she know she was calling a young man recently married, without children, who only had college classes on theology as his background.

I didn't know much in those days about relationships, but in the decades since I have learned a few things. Actually, most people know less about your circumstances and your situation than you do, and their training and ability to help is limited. So here are some guidelines that will help when seeking advice.

When you seek advice, you must make sure that the person is qualified to advise you. The number one qualification is this: does this person have a quality relationship with God, and is the individual sensitive to the leading of the Holy Spirit? How can you determine this about someone else? The Bible says that people will be known by the fruit in their life (Matthew 7:20). In other words, what does the person's life produce? Is the potential counselor faithful and steadfast in his or her own relationships?

I've noticed through the years that there are people who cannot get their own lives organized. These people may have relationship problems with their spouse, their children, and their friends, or maybe they cannot settle into one church, but seem to move from church to church due to the slightest offense. It's amazing, but these kinds of people are all too eager to give advice. Avoid them.

In order to have success in any area, you should never take advice from someone who is a failure in your particular area of need. Wouldn't it be silly for a high school football coach to bring in a coach from a losing team to train his athletes? Of course, it would! So, if you want to improve, always seek advice from someone who has become a victor. An alcoholic would never go down to the back alleys where the drunks are living on the street to get advice on how to be delivered from alcohol. It would be much better for the alcoholic to go to someplace like Alcoholics Anonymous where there is a qualified leader with a room filled with others working to overcome their addictions. Always seek advice on how to be a winner from someone who is successful.

All too often, depressed friends will attempt to bring someone else down to their level so they won't feel as bad about their own situation. The phrase 'misery loves company' is true, but once *misery* and *company* get together, another friend shows up named *destruction*. Many marriages have been broken and lives destroyed because misery and company got together.

When things seem hopeless, there are a lot of places you can go that are filled with people who have given up and lost hope. If your marriage is a mess, and it appears like nothing can be done, stay away from taverns filled with people consuming alcohol in the dark, listening to sad music. Many people surround themselves with friends who think the way they think and who will give them the answers they want to hear. This is a deadly trap that usually doesn't end well. We must know and believe that the Word of God is the ultimate counsel, so associate with friends and counselors who can be trusted to tell the truth.

The Bible says that in the last days there will be those who surround themselves with teachers who will teach them what they want to hear to satisfy their own fleshly lusts (2 Timothy 4:3-4). The only true counsel is the Word of God and those who speak it.

A wise man will hear and increase learning, and a man of understanding will attain wise counsel.

Proverbs 1:5

But there is good news! There are friends and good people who are led by the Spirit of God who desire to help you. If you allow them to speak into your life and submit to their advice, it's amazing how things can start becoming brighter. When a path of recovery or deliverance is revealed through someone else, be careful not to let pride rise up to block your path of deliverance and hope. Receive godly advice to be set free.

Your Inner Circle

When He [Jesus] came into the house, He permitted no one to go in except Peter, James, and John, and the father and mother of the girl.

Luke 8:51

As Jesus traveled doing the work of His ministry, thousands followed Him. As He traveled from town to town, many times He sent a smaller group to visit the town ahead of His arrival so people in the village would know when He would be there. The Bible says this group consisted of seventy people divided into thirty-five groups. But as Jesus entered each town and village to minister, He took with Him His twelve disciples. It seemed like they were continually at His side.

However, there were times when it was extremely important that the only ones around Him were the ones who strongly believed His words. During these times, He distanced Himself from everyone except His inner circle. When He went to pray for Jairus' daughter, He was told she was dead. Instead of filling the room with as many people as possible so He would get more "prayer power," He did just the opposite. He sent everyone out of the room except for those He knew were grounded in His teachings and could be trusted (Luke 8:51).

Likewise, in life everyone knows thousands of people they regularly encounter. But when life and death are in the balance, everyone who is not grounded in the Word should be sent away so only those in the inner circle remain. For this reason, your inner circle cannot include those who speak doubt, unbelief, and discouragement. Without a doubt, the Word of God is true when it says that a wise man will attain wise counsel, but the counsel of fools will bring destruction (Proverbs 13:20).

If you want hope, stop hanging out with the hopeless. In time of need, surround yourself with the promises in the Word of God and with people of faith who are saturated with faith from the inside out and the outside in.

Chapter 9

Biblical Promises that Anchor Your Hope

The key to hope is finding a promise in God's Word that answers what you need, meditating on it, and then standing on the promise. No matter what your circumstances look like, keep standing on God's Word. When God makes a promise and you receive it, you have a covenant with God.

> **This hope we have as an anchor of the soul, both sure and steadfast, and which enters the Presence behind the veil.**
>
> **Hebrews 6:19**

I once heard the story about an experienced sailor who not only knew the ability of his ship and equipment, but also understood how the storms and raging seas could quickly develop without much warning. For this reason, he was always prepared with a tested anchor and line. When he saw a storm approaching, he simply threw out the anchor and secured his boat. He would then go below deck and rest, waiting for the storm to pass.

Every time I think of this story, I am reminded of the life of a Christian. The ship represents our daily lives. The anchor represents the promises of God and the line represents our faith that allows us to be securely connected to the anchor and weather any storm that might come upon us. These promises of God are tested and true so when we believe them, the line connects us securely to them which anchors our life. As a result, we can weather the storm until it passes.

Proving God's Promises

Because of his glory and excellence, He has given us great and precious promises. These are the promises that enable you to share His divine nature and escape the world's corruption caused by human desires.

2 Peter 1:4 (NLT)

There is a difference between testing and proving. A test implies that you are trying something out to see if it works. Many times during the manufacturing of products, a company has an entire department set aside for testing its product. The purpose of the test is to see if the product can sustain the pressures and tensions put upon it. If it doesn't pass the test, the product is refined and upgraded, then retested. In fact, it is tested over and over again until it passes without failing. Once the product passes the testing phase, it's put into use. At this point it is no longer being tested, but it has been proven. By using the product, it now proves that it has passed the previous testing phase.

If you jump out of an airplane with a parachute, you are not testing it to see if it works or not. You believe the line, the material, and the latches have already been tested, so by jumping out of the plane and pulling the rip cord, you are proving that it works. Or when you apply the brakes on your car at an intersection, you are not testing the brakes to see if they function; they have already been tested by the manufacturer. You prove that they work with full knowledge, understanding, and peace that they will stop your car.

Likewise, we don't have to test God's promises to see whether they will work or not. His promises are true, so we should know that His Word is finished and ready for us to implement with our faith. Simply believing in our heart and confessing with our mouth is the work that we must do to prove His Word. We must grasp the concept that God's Word has no tests to pass. His Word is perfect so when it is linked to our faith, it will do exactly what it is sent to do.

> **So shall My word be that goes forth from My mouth; it shall not return to Me void, but it shall accomplish what I please, and it shall prosper in the thing for which I sent it.**
>
> **Isaiah 55:11**

The only reliable, permanent, and unchanging promises we have are the ones from God. When you anchor your hope or tie your hope to anything other than God's promises, you will likely be disappointed because your ship will not be secure. The only way we can withstand the storms of life is to be anchored to His promises. When we throw the anchor overboard, we're not testing it to see if it will work, but we are proving that it does work which enables us to rest during the storm.

What Are the Promises of God?

For all the promises of God in Him are Yes, and in Him Amen, to the glory of God through us.

2 Corinthians 1:20

To begin with, Jesus promised us if we would believe in Him, we would have everlasting life. Paul put it this way. He said that once he believed in Jesus, his old man was crucified with Christ (Romans 6:6). In other words, he proclaimed that death was in his past but not in his future.

As Christians, this alone should be extremely encouraging. We know that for all eternity we will be free and have life, while everything else on earth will have passed into history. We will never die! Our death is not a future event, but has been recorded in our past. However, the promises from God not only apply to our distant future, but they apply to our earthly existence now.

We know that we have an enemy that attacks us in many areas on a daily basis. But the good news is this: for every attack and trial, God has given a promise. These promises are battle-ready for the Christian who believes them in his or her heart and confesses them without wavering. There are literally thousands of promises in God's Word. Obviously they can't all be listed, but here are a few in which you can anchor your hope.

I would also suggest that you be led by the Holy Spirit and choose promises from God that speak to your heart and your situation. Write them down and then meditate on them. They will come alive and minister to you. The Word removes fear and restores hope.

GOD'S PROMISES TO BELIEVERS

Deliverance

His promise: I will not fear. The Lord is with me and goes before me.

And the Lord, He is the One who goes before you. He will be with you, He will not leave you nor forsake you; do not fear nor be dismayed. (Deuteronomy 31:8)

His promise: The Lord is my hiding place. He guards me from trouble.

You are my hiding place; You shall preserve me from trouble; You shall surround me with songs of deliverance. (Psalm 32:7)

His promise: The Lord rescues me from death.

He rescues them from death and keeps them alive in times of famine. (Psalm 33:19)

His promise: The Lord delivers me from all my fears.

I sought the Lord, and He heard me, and delivered me from all my fears. (Psalm 34:4)

His promise: The Lord delivers me out of every affliction.

Many are the afflictions of the righteous, but the Lord delivers him out of them all. (Psalm 34:19)

His promise: The Lord will deliver me in the day of trouble and I will glorify Him.

Call upon Me in the day of trouble; I will deliver you, and you shall glorify Me. (Psalm 50:15)

His promise: The Lord delivered me out of my desperate circumstances.

Then they cried out to the Lord in their trouble, and He delivered them out of their distresses. (Psalm 107:6)

His promise: The Lord is with me to deliver me, even when I am old.

Even to your old age, I am He, and even to gray hairs I will carry you! I have made, and I will bear; even I will carry, and will deliver you. (Isaiah 46:4)

His promise: God gives me the victory.

But thanks be to God, who gives us the victory through our Lord Jesus Christ. (1 Corinthians 15:57)

His promise: The Lord will deliver me from every evil work.

And the Lord will deliver me from every evil work and preserve me for His heavenly kingdom. (2 Timothy 4:18)

His promise: When I submit to God and resist the devil, he will flee.

Therefore submit to God. Resist the devil and he will flee from you. (James 4:7)

His promise: I am an overcomer, because greater is He that is in me than he that is in the world.

You are of God, little children, and have overcome them, because He who is in you is greater than he who is in the world. (1 John 4:4)

Health and Healing

His promise: God heals me.

I am the Lord who heals you. (Exodus 15:26)

His promise: He heals all my diseases.

Who forgives all your iniquities, who heals all your diseases. (Psalm 103:3)

His promise: He sent His Word to heal me and deliver me.

He sent His word and healed them, and delivered them from their destructions. (Psalm 107:20 NIV)

His promise: I will not die, but live.

I will not die; instead, I will live to tell what the Lord has done. (Psalm 118:17 NLT)

His promise: His Word is health to my flesh.

My son, give attention to my words; incline your ear to my sayings. Do not let them depart from your eyes; keep them in the midst of your heart; for they are life to those who find them, and health to all their flesh. (Proverbs 4:20-22)

His promise: Kind words are healthy for my body.

Kind words are like honey — sweet to the soul and healthy for the body. (Proverbs 16:24 NLT)

His promise: He bore my sickness for me.

That it might be fulfilled which was spoken by Isaiah the prophet, saying: "He Himself took our infirmities and bore our sicknesses." (Matthew 8:17)

His promise: Jesus came to heal my broken heart, therefore my heart is healed.

The Spirit of the Lord is upon Me, because He has anointed Me to preach the gospel to the poor; He has sent Me to heal the brokenhearted. (Luke 4:18)

His promise: The same Spirit that raised Jesus dwells in me and gives life to my mortal body.

But if the Spirit of Him who raised Jesus from the dead dwells in you, He who raised Christ from the dead will also give life to your mortal bodies through His Spirit who dwells in you. (Romans 8:11)

His promise: The prayer of faith will heal me.

Is anyone among you sick? Let him call for the elders of the church, and let them pray over him, anointing him with oil in the name of the Lord. And the prayer of faith will save the sick, and the Lord will raise him up. And if he has committed sins, he will be forgiven. (James 5:14-15)

His promise: By His stripes I have been healed.

He Himself bore our sins in His own body on the tree, that we, having died to sins, might live for righteousness—by whose stripes you were healed. (1 Peter 2:24)

Children and Grandchildren

His promise: His mercy is on my grandchildren.

But the mercy of the LORD is from everlasting to everlasting on those who fear Him, and His righteousness to children's children. (Psalm 103:17)

His promise: My household is blessed.

Praise the LORD! Blessed is the man who fears the LORD, who delights greatly in His commandments. His descendants will be mighty on earth; the generation of the upright will be blessed. (Psalm 112:1-2)

His promise: My children will not be put to shame.

Like arrows in the hands of a warrior are children born in one's youth. Blessed is the man whose quiver is full of them. They will not be put to shame when they contend with their opponents in court. (Psalm 127:4-5 NIV)

His promise: My children and grandchildren will be delivered.

Though they join forces, the wicked will not go unpunished; but the posterity (descendants) of the righteous will be delivered. (Proverbs 11:21)

His promise: My children are blessed.

The righteous man walks in his integrity; his children are blessed after him. (Proverbs 20:7)

His promise: My time is not wasted in training my child.

Train up a child in the way he should go, and when he is old he will not depart from it. (Proverbs 22:6)

His promise: When I speak God's Word, so will my children and grandchildren.

"As for Me," says the Lord, "this is My covenant with them: My Spirit who is upon you, and My words which I have put in your mouth, shall not depart from your mouth, nor from the mouth of your descendants, nor from the mouth of your descendants' descendants," says the Lord, "from this time and forevermore." (Isaiah 59:21)

His promise: God will teach my children and they will have great peace.

All your children shall be taught by the Lord, and great shall be the peace of your children. (Isaiah 54:13)

Wisdom

His promise: When I ask, God generously gives me wisdom.

If any of you lacks wisdom, you should ask God, who gives generously to all without finding fault, and it will be given to you. (James 1:5 NIV)

His promise: My wisdom comes from above.

But the wisdom that is from above is first pure, then peaceable, gentle, willing to yield, full of mercy and good fruits, without partiality and without hypocrisy. (James 3:17)

Protection

His promise: The Lord will fight for me.

The Lord will fight for you, and you shall hold your peace. (Exodus 14:14)

His promise: I will not be afraid, because He will never leave me or forsake me.

Be strong and of good courage, do not fear nor be afraid of them; for the Lord your God, He is the One who goes with you. He will not leave you nor forsake you. (Deuteronomy 31:6)

His promise: I put my trust in Him and He defends me.

But let all those rejoice who put their trust in You; let them ever shout for joy, because You defend them; let those also who love Your name be joyful in You. (Psalm 5:11)

His promise: The Lord is my shelter and security in times of trouble.

The Lord also will be a refuge for the oppressed, a refuge in times of trouble. (Psalm 9:9)

His promise: The Lord protects me from evil people.

"Because the poor are plundered and the needy groan, I will now arise," says the Lord. "I will protect them from those who malign them." (Psalm 12:5 NIV)

His promise: The Lord will save me from my enemies.

I will call upon the Lord, who is worthy to be praised; so shall I be saved from my enemies. (Psalm 18:3)

His promise: I have no reason to be afraid because the Lord is my strength.

The Lord is my light and my salvation; whom shall I fear? The Lord is the strength of my life; of whom shall I be afraid? (Psalm 27:1)

His promise: In times of trouble, He will hide me in His secret place.

For in the time of trouble He shall hide me in His pavilion; in the secret place of His tabernacle He shall hide me; He shall set me high upon a rock. (Psalm 27:5)

His promise: I shall not be condemned.

The Lord redeems the soul of His servants, and none of those who trust in Him shall be condemned. (Psalm 34:22)

His promise: God is my help in times of trouble.

God is our refuge and strength, a very present help in trouble. (Psalm 46:1)

His promise: God is my place of safety until all the calamities have passed.

Be merciful to me, O God, be merciful to me! For my soul trusts in You; and in the shadow of Your wings I will make my refuge, until these calamities have passed by. (Psalm 57:1)

His promise: The Lord is my hiding place and my shield.

You are my hiding place and my shield; I hope in Your word. (Psalm 119:114)

His promise: My help comes from the Lord.

I will lift up my eyes to the hills—from whence comes my help? My help comes from the Lord, Who made heaven and earth. (Psalm 121:1-2)

His promise: The Lord will keep me from evil and protect me when I travel.

The Lord shall preserve you from all evil; He shall preserve your soul. The Lord shall preserve your going out and your coming in from this time forth, and even forevermore. (Psalm 121:7-8)

His promise: In the middle of trouble, He will save me.

Though I walk in the midst of trouble, You will revive me; You will stretch out Your hand against the wrath of my enemies, and Your right hand will save me. (Psalm 138:7)

His promise: His name protects me like a strong tower.

The name of the Lord is a strong tower; the righteous run to it and are safe. (Proverbs 18:10)

His promise: The Lord protects me from harm.

Fear of the Lord leads to life, bringing security and protection from harm. (Proverbs 19:23 NLT)

His promise: When I am in a difficult situation, the Lord will protect me.

When you pass through the waters, I will be with you; and through the rivers, they shall not overflow you. When you walk through the fire, you shall not be burned, nor shall the flame scorch you. (Isaiah 43:2)

His promise: No weapon formed against me will prosper. Words spoken against me will be proved to be wrong. This is my heritage.

"No weapon formed against you shall prosper, and every tongue which rises against you in judgment you shall condemn. This is the heritage of the servants of the Lord, and their righteousness is from Me," says the Lord. (Isaiah 54:17)

His promise: God is for me. It doesn't matter who is against me.

What then shall we say to these things? If God is for us, who can be against us? (Romans 8:31)

His promise: Even when things are very difficult, I am not destroyed.

We are hard-pressed on every side, yet not crushed; we are perplexed, but not in despair; persecuted, but not forsaken; struck down, but not destroyed. (2 Corinthians 4:8-9)

His promise: The Lord strengthens me and protects me from the evil one.

But the Lord is faithful, and he will strengthen you and protect you from the evil one. (2 Thessalonians 3:3 NIV)

His promise: The Lord is my helper. I will not fear.

So we may boldly say: "The Lord is my helper; I will not fear. What can man do to me?" (Hebrews 13:6)

Peace

His promise: Because I trust in the Lord, I have peace.

You will keep him in perfect peace, whose mind is stayed on You, because he trusts in You. (Isaiah 26:3)

His promise: God gives me supernatural peace.

Peace I leave with you, My peace I give to you; not as the world gives do I give to you. Let not your heart be troubled, neither let it be afraid. (John 14:27)

His promise: I have peace because He has overcome the world.

These things I have spoken to you, that in Me you may have peace. In the world you will have tribulation; but be of good cheer, I have overcome the world. (John 16:33)

His promise: I have peace that surpasses understanding.

Be anxious for nothing, but in everything by prayer and supplication, with thanksgiving, let your requests be made known to God; and the peace of God, which surpasses all understanding, will guard your hearts and minds through Christ Jesus. (Philippians 4:6-7)

His promise: My heart is at peace.

Let the peace of Christ rule in your hearts, since as members of one body you were called to peace. And be thankful. (Colossians 3:15 NIV)

His promise: I am a peacemaker.

Now the fruit of righteousness is sown in peace by those who make peace. (James 3:18)

Strength

His promise: The Lord gives me strength and peace.

The Lord will give strength to His people; the Lord will bless His people with peace. (Psalm 29:11)

His promise: Even when I am weak, the Lord increases my strength.

He gives power to the weak, and to those who have no might He increases strength. (Isaiah 40:29)

His promise: God will strengthen me and help me.

Fear not, for I am with you; be not dismayed, for I am your God. I will strengthen you, yes, I will help you, I will uphold you with My righteous right hand. (Isaiah 41:10)

Rest

His promise: I can safely lay down in peace and sleep.

I will both lie down in peace, and sleep; for You alone, O Lord, make me dwell in safety. (Psalm 4:8)

His promise: My mind is at rest.

Yes, my soul, find rest in God; my hope comes from Him. (Psalm 62:5 NIV)

His promise: He loves me and grants sleep to me.

In vain you rise early and stay up late, toiling for food to eat—for he grants sleep to those he loves. (Psalm 127:2)

His promise: My soul is at rest.

Come to Me, all you who labor and are heavy laden, and I will give you rest. Take My yoke upon you and learn from Me, for I am gentle and lowly in heart, and you will find rest for your souls. (Matthew 11:28-29)

His promise: I choose to enter His rest.

There remains therefore a rest for the people of God. (Hebrews 4:9)

Prosperity

His promise: Whatever I do will prosper.

He shall be like a tree planted by the rivers of water, that brings forth its fruit in its season, whose leaf also shall not wither; and whatever he does shall prosper. (Psalm 1:3)

His promise: God takes pleasure in my prosperity.

Let them shout for joy and be glad, who favor my righteous cause; and let them say continually, "Let the Lord be magnified, Who has pleasure in the prosperity of His servant." (Psalm 35:27)

His promise: My children are not beggars, but are blessed.

I have been young, and now am old; yet I have not seen the righteous forsaken, nor his descendants begging bread. He is ever merciful, and lends; and his descendants are blessed. (Psalm 37:25-26)

His promise: God is not withholding any good thing from me.

For the Lord God is a sun and shield; the Lord will give grace and glory; no good thing will He withhold from those who walk uprightly. (Psalm 84:11)

His promise: God makes me prosperous without sorrow.

The blessing of the Lord makes one rich, and He adds no sorrow with it. (Proverbs 10:22)

His promise: My generosity will prosper me.

A generous person will prosper; whoever refreshes others will be refreshed. (Proverbs 11:25 NIV)

His promise: My trust in the Lord assures prosperity in my life.

The greedy stir up conflict, but those who trust in the Lord will prosper. (Proverbs 28:25 NIV)

His promise: Jesus took on poverty so I can have prosperity.

For you know the grace of our Lord Jesus Christ, that though He was rich, yet for your sakes He became poor, that you through His poverty might become rich. (2 Corinthians 8:9 NIV)

God's Plan for My Life

His promise: God has a good plan for my life.

For I know the thoughts that I think toward you, says the Lord, thoughts of peace and not of evil, to give you a future and a hope. (Jeremiah 29:11)

His promise: My life is recorded in God's book. He has a plan for my life.

You saw me before I was born. Every day of my life was recorded in your book. Every moment was laid out before a single day had passed. (Psalm 139:16 NLT)

Food, Clothing, and Housing

His promise: God will provide my clothing.

Now if God so clothes the grass of the field, which today is, and tomorrow is thrown into the oven, will He not much more clothe you, O you of little faith? (Matthew 6:30)

His promise: God will provide food and clothing for me.

But seek first the kingdom of God and His righteousness, and all these things shall be added to you. (Matthew 6:33)

His promise: God supplies bread for food.

Now he who supplies seed to the sower and bread for food will also supply and increase your store of seed and will enlarge the harvest of your righteousness. (2 Corinthians 9:10 NIV)

His promise: I will dwell safely without fear.

But whoever listens to me will dwell safely, and will be secure, without fear of evil. (Proverbs 1:33)

His promise: My home is peaceful, secure, and quiet.

My people will dwell in a peaceful habitation, in secure dwellings, and in quiet resting places. (Isaiah 32:18)

His promise: My house and food will not be stolen.

They shall build houses and inhabit them; they shall plant vineyards and eat their fruit. They shall not build and another inhabit; they shall not plant and another eat; for as the days of a tree, so shall be the days of My people, and My elect shall long enjoy the work of their hands. (Isaiah 65:21-22)

Eternal Life

His promise: God sent Jesus for me. I have everlasting life.

For God so loved the world that He gave His only begotten Son, that whoever believes in Him should not perish but have everlasting life. (John 3:16)

His promise: Eternal life is God's gift to me.

For the wages of sin is death, but the gift of God is eternal life in Christ Jesus our Lord. (Romans 6:23)

God's Promises Are for You

Some of the above promises were spoken to the Hebrews who were the natural seed of Abraham. However, never forget this: if you are a born-again Christian, saved by faith through grace, then the promises to the seed of Abraham are also for you.

> That the blessing of Abraham might come upon the Gentiles in Christ Jesus, that we might receive the promise of the Spirit through faith.
>
> Galatians 3:14

> If you are Christ's, then you are Abraham's seed, and heirs according to the promise.
>
> Galatians 3:29

More Promises of Encouragement from the Word

His promise: I will lay hands on the sick and they will recover.

And these signs will follow those who believe: In My name they will cast out demons; they will speak with new tongues; they will take up serpents; and if they drink anything deadly, it will by no means hurt them; they will lay hands on the sick, and they will recover. (Mark 16:17-18)

His promise: I have received the Holy Spirit because I asked.

If you then, being evil, know how to give good gifts to your children, how much more will your heavenly Father give the Holy Spirit to those who ask Him! (Luke 11:13)

His promise: I am free because Jesus has made me free.

Therefore if the Son makes you free, you shall be free indeed. (John 8:36)

His promise: The Holy Spirit will guide me into truth and will tell me things to come.

When He, the Spirit of truth, has come, He will guide you into all truth; for He will not speak on His own authority, but whatever He hears He will speak; and He will tell you things to come. (John 16:13)

His promise: When I need to love others, I remember that the love of God has been poured out in my heart by the Holy Spirit.

Now hope does not disappoint, because the love of God has been poured out in our hearts by the Holy Spirit who was given to us. (Romans 5:5)

His promise: The law of the Spirit of life has made me free from the law of sin and death.

For the law of the Spirit of life in Christ Jesus has made me free from the law of sin and death. (Romans 8:2)

His promise: All things work together for my good.

And we know that all things work together for good to those who love God, to those who are the called according to His purpose. (Romans 8:28)

His promise: I am blessed with every spiritual blessing in the heavenly places.

Blessed be the God and Father of our Lord Jesus Christ, who has blessed us with every spiritual blessing in the heavenly places in Christ. (Ephesians 1:3)

His promise: In Him I have redemption and forgiveness.

In Him we have redemption through His blood, the forgiveness of sins, according to the riches of His grace. (Ephesians 1:7)

His promise: In Him I have obtained an inheritance.

In Him also we have obtained an inheritance, being predestined according to the purpose of Him who works all things according to the counsel of His will. (Ephesians 1:11)

His promise: I am sealed with the Holy Spirit, who is the guarantee of my inheritance.

In Him you also trusted, after you heard the word of truth, the gospel of your salvation; in whom also, having believed, you were sealed with the Holy Spirit of promise, who is the guarantee of our inheritance until the redemption of the purchased possession, to the praise of His glory. (Ephesians 1:13-14)

His promise: God shall supply all my need according to His riches.

And my God shall supply all your need according to His riches in glory by Christ Jesus. (Philippians 4:19)

His promise: I am content because He will never leave me nor forsake me.

Let your conduct be without covetousness; be content with such things as you have. For He Himself has said, "I will never leave you nor forsake you." (Hebrews 13:5)

His promise: I am an overcomer. I overcome the enemy by the blood of the Lamb and the word of my testimony.

And they overcame him by the blood of the Lamb and by the word of their testimony, and they did not love their lives to the death. (Revelation 12:11)

Chapter 10

Natural Steps to Hope

Secular books about hope often contain no reference to the promises of God or anything Christian for that matter. While these books may help to a degree, we must never forget that any permanent solution to any problem must be rooted and grounded spiritually. However, natural remedies cannot be ignored, because they have value.

In this chapter, you will find practical ideas you can put into practice that will help build up your hope while eliminating discouragement and hopelessness. While the principles have a spiritual as well as natural application, they will vary from person to person depending upon the circumstances of life.

You may feel that some of them are impossible for you to accomplish, but that is not true. You may hear a voice of discouragement telling you that you cannot do these things, but it is not from God. Rather, it is rooted in the evil side of the spirit realm that seeks defeat in your life. Do not listen to these voices!

They may come as thoughts or actual words from another person, but take them captive and cast them down (2 Corinthians 10:5). Instead, choose to believe the truth, and the truth is this: as a Christian, you have been empowered by the Holy Spirit to do the impossible. Regardless of how it may appear, you have been given complete authority and control over your own life and destiny.

Practical Ideas

The following practical ideas will guide you as the Holy Spirit reveals to you the application for them in your life. A more detailed explanation of these ideas follow this list.

Renew your relationship with God

- Meditate on His Word
- See your future as God sees it
- Revisit your dream
- Think about the possibilities of success
- Spend time in His presence

Create a fresh, positive atmosphere

- Turn on the lights
- Reject oppressive culture
- Create an atmosphere for hope

Take care of your body

- Get physical exercise
- Expose yourself to sunlight

- Get enough sleep
- Eat healthy
- Take a shower, brush your teeth, comb your hair, put on clean clothes
- Surround yourself with a neat and clean environment

Guard your eyes and ears
- Listen to uplifting music—avoid sad and depressing songs
- Take a 30-day Christian music challenge

Develop a positive mental attitude
- Build on the truth
- Get mental exercise
- Avoid negative mental bullies

Develop healthy associations
- Learn not to let discouraging words penetrate your heart
- Talk it out with a friend or Christian counselor
- Monitor your friendships
- Quit hanging out with the "you'll-never-make-it" crowd
- Never take advice from fools

Change your speech
- Quit speaking death into your dream
- Quit making excuses
- Start declaring, "I can" and "I will"

Develop a permanent, positive pattern of living

- Set a life pattern
- Get into a routine
- Set goals
- Take on responsibilities
- Be thankful
- Make time to praise and worship God
- Find a home church
- Try to have fun
- Do something new
- Help someone else

Develop a hobby

- Get a pet, take care of plants, or find something to do that requires you to get off the couch

Be cautious about using medication

- Always seek professional advice before taking drugs or supplements

Prepare for the realization of your hope

- Beware of the imaginary barrier
- Maintain a lifestyle of hope

Renew Your Relationship with God

While hopelessness and depression manifest themselves physically, the source of each of these is spiritual, and spiritual attacks must have a spiritual solution. Jesus said that we must seek first God's kingdom and His righteousness before physical relief is received (Matthew 6:33). So in order to eliminate hopelessness, first and foremost you must renew and refresh your relationship with God. Otherwise any relief is temporary.

Renewing your relationship involves several things. First, you must make the decision to believe everything He says while seeing things the way He sees them. More specifically, you must see yourself as He sees you. As you meditate on His Word and spend time worshiping Him, the Holy Spirit will impart to you His revelation and plan for your life. See your future as God sees it. Without a close relationship with God, it is impossible to have clear direction for your future.

Sometimes when we have a goal or a dream, as time passes, our fleshly nature tends to let it fade. Sometimes we even create false memories of what God has spoken to us. That's why it is so important to write down your goals and dreams (Habakkuk 2:2). After all, that's what God did. He wrote His plan for man in a Book so the plan can be visualized as well as completed. As you regularly revisit your goals and dreams, it will keep your hope alive. As you think about the possibilities of success, your hope will increase.

So when you are feeling burdened by the cares of life and it seems as though you've lost your direction, revisit God's promise to you—the one written in His Word and written in your heart by the revelation of the Holy Spirit. Revisiting the promise will refuel the hope, igniting excitement for the good God has placed before you.

One of the most healing things you can do is to have the Spirit of God minister to you. This happens when you get into

His presence, and music can be a very powerful vehicle to get you there. Find a good source for worship songs. Listen to them and worship Him. In His presence you will find healing, joy, and everything else you need (Psalm 16:11).

Create a Fresh Positive Atmosphere

The kingdom of light and the kingdom of darkness are opposites. The Bible says God is light and in Him is no darkness at all (1 John 1:5). The demonic presence of evil (darkness) leaves when the glorious presence of God (light) is present. This is a spiritual principle that is mirrored in the realm of our physical existence. Light always overpowers darkness spiritually as well as physically. Darkness is the absence of light. To make room for the darkness, you must shut out the light.

Using this principle in the physical realm is extremely important. One of the first steps in defeating depression and hopelessness is to simply open the curtains and let the light in. If it is night, turn on the lights. Most psychologists believe that our thinking becomes brighter as our surroundings become brighter. So when heaviness or hopelessness come knocking at your door, surround yourself with the spiritual light of God's Word and turn on the lights. Pull back the curtains, open the windows, and take a deep breath of fresh air! It will do wonders for your attitude.

Reject Oppressive Culture

When one of my granddaughters was in preschool, she asked me if I could remember the Civil War. It made me realize that historical events for the younger generation sometimes seem to flow together. So for a moment, I will enlighten you on what it was like to grow up as a teenager in the 1960s.

At the beginning of the decade, the main music style was rock 'n roll with many young men and women becoming famous singing this style of music. As the decade began, these musicians usually performed in suit and tie. Even though the older generation didn't like the rock 'n roll sound, it had a somewhat clean and youthful innocence to it. But as the decade progressed, several things took place that seemed as though they were all happening at once.

First, the President of the United States, John F. Kennedy, was assassinated. Then the Vietnam War became a very prominent point of protest across the United States, and the music style changed as British bands—the Beatles, the Rolling Stones, Herman's Hermits, as well as many other British musicians— took over the music industry. The young people living during this decade were the largest youth group the world had ever seen, and it was nicknamed the *Baby Boomers,* since they were all born shortly after the end of World War II.

With riots and war protests came cultural changes. Many young people either entered fully into this change or, at the very minimum, wore the clothing styles and took on the actions of those who became known as "hippies." This Baby Boomer generation that embraced the hippy lifestyle immersed itself in this new culture that included lava lamps, incense, bell bottoms, drugs, and British rock 'n roll.

The previous generation left farms and factories all across America to fight the Nazis in World War II. They have been called the Great Generation. This generation was generally a Bible-believing, conservative group who believed in hard work and a no-nonsense approach to life and to church. I'm quite sure they were bewildered when they saw their children heading off to Woodstock!

During this decade, extreme cultural changes were taking place throughout the world. While there was great searching by this Baby Boomer generation for truth, it also opened the door for demonic influence. Even though it is true that we should search for truth, we should never forget that all truth originates with the Word of God. When you open your consciousness and your heart to any spiritual philosophy or spiritual cult, the forces of darkness are all too eager to present mysticism as well as false doctrines that lead to destruction.

When a person is in a hopeless state or they feel there is no escape from their dilemma, they can often become extremely susceptible to any spark of deliverance, regardless of its source. This is why any group that promises peace, joy, and hope that is not grounded in the true Word of God should be avoided at all costs. These false cults are traps of the enemy waiting for someone to become so hopeless that they can be ensnared or trapped, with the end being destruction (2 Peter 2:1).

Create an Atmosphere for Hope

I was a typical young person growing up during that time, wanting to have friends and feel like I fit in. But from an early age I knew there was a calling of God on my life. I tried to fit in, but I was always different. When my friends had spiritual questions, it seemed that I was the one they always came to. Even though I tried to dress like and act like the other young people of the day, when a crisis occurred, I was usually the one they contacted for help or counsel.

It was during this time I remember getting a call at my house from a friend. My friend's words were slurred and difficult to understand. He talked about "ending it all because life isn't worth living." I told him to stay where he was and not to do anything until I got there.

Upon arriving at his apartment about thirty minutes later, I found him in a dark room with incense burning and psychedelic music blasting in the background. Many musicians acknowledged that psychedelic music was frequently recorded while the musicians were on drugs. Many ministers called the music satanic. With this music blaring in my friend's darkened room along with incense burning, the stage was set for destruction.

Immediately I began to reverse the destructive atmosphere. I turned off the music, unplugged the lava lamp, put out the incense, turned on the lights, and then I began the process of counseling my friend. I believe his life was saved that day. Although the first things I did were merely physical changes (music, lights, and fragrance), their removal created the atmosphere for deliverance.

That brings me to this reality. One of the first things that must be done to bring hope to people is to remove the atmosphere of hopelessness. In order to do this, there must be physical changes. Sometimes the changes need to be sight, sound, and smell. In other cases, the changes may need to be friends and location or even a combination of several different things. Whatever the case may be, there must be a change from the atmosphere of darkness to the liberty of light. Don't allow the light to be blocked!

Take Care of Your Body

God created our bodies in such a way that physical exercise produces endorphins which in turn affect our mental attitude, relieving both physical tension and stress. Depression is enhanced by darkness, but joy comes in the morning (Psalm 30:5). Put on your walking shoes, go outside and take a walk. Sunshine is required for good health. Do something physical within the natural limits of your body. Remember to drink plenty of water so you don't become dehydrated.

There are several practical things that you can do physically that will change your attitude. Some may even seem like they have no connection to hopelessness, but as you begin to take care of yourself physically, it will affect you mentally as well as emotionally.

You must eat right and get enough sleep. Eating healthy involves things like choosing whole fresh foods while avoiding processed food as much as possible. Don't skip meals or overeat, both of which are extremes. The timing of your meals is also important. I've heard it said, "If you ate after eight, then you ate too late." Common sense will go a long way with your healthy eating habits. Avoid thinking, *This won't hurt me this one time!* because that line of thinking can be thought every time!

Even personal hygiene will affect your attitude. Take a shower, brush your teeth, comb your hair, and put on clean clothes!

Also, make your bed every morning, take out the trash, wash the dishes, and hang up your clothes and towels. When you are surrounded by a neat and clean environment, a certain level of irritability will be eliminated.

This neat environment should not be restricted to only your home, but should also include your automobile and your desk at work. I'm not suggesting that your desk have no papers on it, because a busy person usually has several stacks. And I'm not saying that your car will always look spotless, especially if you have children or grandkids. But what I am saying is this: a car that is continually full of trash, a messy desk with a computer keyboard that is never cleaned, and a house or apartment where the trash piles up or the sink is continually full of dirty dishes does not create an atmosphere that is refreshing. And if your life feels hopeless, you need to be living in a refreshing atmosphere.

Guard Your Eyes and Ears

Your eyes and your ears are the gateway to your soul. The images you see and the words you hear enter like seeds in a garden that grow beautiful flowers or ugly weeds. What grows in your mind is determined by the seed you allow to be planted. It is true that you cannot control everything you see or everything you hear, but that cannot be used as an excuse to accept every image or word. If the words you are hearing are not words that build up, but instead are words that destroy, then you must find the source of those words and move your listening device (your ears) as far away as possible.

Words you receive will grow into freshness, freedom, and hope, or they will grow into weeds and thorns that will choke and destroy the freshness you need. Continually hearing destructive words will leave your mind as hardened, cracked ground with no life, just like a desert. This makes it difficult to receive anything. You must guard what you hear!

A bomb is a very destructive device and standing next to it when it explodes can be deadly. But the farther away you get from the bomb, the less impact it will have on you. Words are much the same way. Distance yourself from the source of destructive words. If someone else's mouth is the "bomb" in your life, then you must distance yourself from their mouth.

Movies and various types of entertainment can be uplifting or depressive. The movies you watch as well as the theatrical performances you attend are totally at your discretion. You should choose them with an attitude of godliness.

Once a man who had attended a theatrical performance recommended it to me. But he said, "You won't want to take your children though, because the performance has several nude scenes." I told him that not only would I not take my children, but I would not go myself or take my wife because I did not want my family exposed to public nudity. I was shocked when he replied to me, "But this is different because it is artistic."

One of the greatest deceptions with sin is when people quit calling it sin and call it art, or expression, or talent. Likewise, you cannot allow negativity or depressive words of defeat to enter your ears because someone presents it to you as information. Do not be deceived. Changing the name of the content does not change the content!

Take a 30-Day Christian Music Challenge

Music existed even before the creation of man. Its original purpose was for the heavenly hosts and all of creation to worship God. On earth, musical instruments and voices can create many different styles and melodies. As I've traveled around the world, it seems that most nations have their own unique musical style. In some countries there are even different styles within the nation.

But regardless of where you live, music itself has the innate ability to lift you to a higher level or to bring you down. Because music has the ability to deeply affect you within your soul emotionally, you must not allow yourself to feed on music that amplifies your despair, loneliness, or hopelessness.

If you are depressed or you feel like there's nothing in life left for you, then I would suggest not listening to B.B. King singing, "The Thrill is Gone," but instead you should listen to Edwin Hawkins singing, "Oh Happy Day." If you don't want to be sorrowful, listen to uplifting music, not sad or depressing songs. It's like the old computer programming phrase: "garbage in—garbage out!"

Think about the music you listen to and purposely choose to change so you hear only music that uplifts you. The music you listen to is a big deal because it gets in your soul. Check out Christian radio or apps that play positive inspiring music that's full of hope.

Much of today's secular music culture is filled with filthy, degrading, unhealthy lyrics that fill your mind with dark thoughts and perverted concepts. Don't make the mistake of thinking you have to put up with it just because you like the style of music.

There is a whole new generation of Christian artists today that produce wholesome, positive upbeat Christian music rivaling anything in the secular music industry. With styles from traditional to Southern gospel, from adult contemporary to various genres of rock, and more, it's a new world in Christian music. Most of the songs on today's Christian radio stations sing about the hope, forgiveness, and change that comes from knowing God and knowing He has the answers to your problems.

Even if you don't have a local Christian radio station, because of the Internet you can listen online to virtually any Christian radio station anywhere in the world. Take the challenge of listening only to Christian music for 30 days and see what it does to your attitude.

Develop a Positive Mental Attitude

In the Bible, find the promise of God that specifically addresses your particular problem and put on a full court press to get it in your soul by meditating on it, keeping it before your eyes, talking about it, listening to teachers who teach about it, and saturating your entire soul with the promise. Build on the truth as you get it into the different parts of your soul—your mind, will, and emotions.

How do you saturate each one of these parts of your soul? Saturate your mind and intellect by constantly hearing it. Saturate your emotions by dreaming about it and by fantasizing what it will be like to be delivered. Imagine seeing yourself in the end result of the full manifestation. Saturate your will by speaking what you want out loud to yourself and to other people. It doesn't matter if other people think you are crazy! It matters whether or not you believe, speak the promise, and imagine that promise being fulfilled.

Get Mental Exercise

Mental exercise is the act of applying your thinking power to a project, puzzle, or pastime which focuses your problem-solving abilities on something other than the stress or depression you are currently feeling in life. As you refocus your thoughts on something that is different or somewhat challenging, it will take the focus away from your troubles. Unfortunately, when pressures of life or disenchantment with life seem overpowering, to even attempt to refocus sometimes does not seem desirable. Here you have another choice to make.

For some, the choice may be to play solitaire or work a puzzle. One elderly gentleman I knew told me that when the pressures of his business became so great that he felt himself becoming overwhelmed and wanting to escape, he would go into the company break room with a notepad to work mathematical equations. For him, as he intently focused on the equations, his business problems faded into the background, giving him a break from the pressure.

The bottom line is this. Instead of being weighed down by constantly dwelling on the problem, refocus your mind on something that actually requires some depth of thinking, which can be a great natural stress reliever.

Avoid Negative Mental Bullies

Everyone has encountered bullies during their lifetime. When I was a young teenager, I had a black leather jacket and a long silk white scarf. It was the style of the day for those who were "cool." One day at school, a bully took my scarf. He was older, more muscular, and had the ability. He had no regard for me or my feelings. Although that was many years ago, to this day I can still remember the feeling I had when this bully pushed me, pulled my white silk scarf from around my neck and walked away with it, claiming it as his own.

As I grew older and taller, rarely did I again encounter anyone who was a physical bully to me, although I have noticed throughout my life that there are many who are verbal bullies. This kind of bully attempts, through their words of intimidation, to manipulate and control others. Sadly, there are many who fall prey to these manipulative and controlling people and live their lives under the pressure and control of someone else. These controlling people may be in the workplace, at school, in your neighborhood, or in your house, but regardless of who they are, their influence is rarely positive in any way. Their overbearing presence, if tolerated, can beat down and inhibit the controlled person from true expression.

In order to anticipate and expect your hopes and dreams to come to pass, you must be free from the bondage of being controlled by the overpowering personality of others. While they may attempt to control your thoughts through bullying or pressure, ultimately you are in control of your own thoughts. Choose your thoughts wisely.

Develop Healthy Associations

There may be situations when you are unable to eliminate the presence of a person who is a negative influence, one who continually ridicules or belittles your God-given dream. In cases like this, you must train yourself to ignore the words of defeat that you are constantly hearing. This person may be a boss, a supervisor, or a co-worker and you may be unable to work out of their presence or transfer to another department or job. They might be a family member or even a spouse, but regardless of the source, you cannot allow discouraging words to penetrate your heart. This is when you must have a strong shield of faith that can quench the fiery darts of doubt and unbelief that are constantly being hurled at you (Ephesians 6:16).

You must build godly relationships and sever unhealthy relationships to the best of your ability. Relationships involve conversation, and conversation usually brings advice. So you must monitor your friendships. Seek out godly friends or godly Christian counselors who can help you talk it out. The source of all your advice must be positive and line up with the Word of God. While secular counseling may accomplish some things, it can never accomplish what spiritual counseling through the Word of God can do. When you surround yourself with people who know the Word in their heart, that's primarily the type of counsel they will give.

The Bible says death and life are in the power of the tongue (Proverbs 18:21). This statement from the Word of God can be better understood if you make it personal: "My death and my life are in the power of my tongue." While this is a true statement that must be understood, it is also true that your life and your death can be in the power of the tongue of those you associate with if you continue to allow their words to be spoken in your presence. It's difficult to be a positive person if your friends are negative. Quit hanging out with the "you'll-never-make-it" crowd.

Never Take Advice from Fools

Several years ago, I counseled a man who was happily engaged to the love of his life. He had known his fiancée since high school and they had always been close. But a few months before their wedding, he abruptly told her he did not want to get married, but he would welcome the idea of her moving into his apartment to live with him indefinitely. She was a godly girl who had been raised in a conservative church that had very high moral standards. She was a good Christian, and because of this, she declined his offer.

As the months went by, she met another young man in her church who likewise had high moral standards. He proposed, she accepted and a wedding date was set. The young man who was counseling with me was devastated. He asked me, "How could this happen? How could she reject me and fall in love with another man?" Of course, I told him that she didn't reject him but rather he had left her no choice.

Then I asked him this question. I said, "You have always been a man of godly principles. You were raised in the church and, as far as I know, you have always believed that a man and woman should be married before they lived together. Your parents are happily married, so what gave you the idea that you and your fiancée should live together without getting married?"

He looked at me with a puzzled look and I could see his wheels were turning. He was asking himself, why? Then he came up with this explanation. He said, "The men that I work with decided to give me a bachelor's party. At the party, we stayed up most of the night talking about marriage. Every one of them told me that marriage would destroy the relationship with my fiancée, so the only way to keep a good relationship with her was to avoid marriage. One of them even said to me, 'Why buy the cow when the milk's free?'"

I sat there in disbelief wanting to shake my head, but I knew that would not be a good thing to do. I had known this man for years, and I thought he was smarter than that. He had made a major life decision based upon the words of his associates who did not know his fiancée and who had no vested interest in his life. His decision did not affect them in any way. They were worldly people who did not know or live by the principles in the Word of God. They may have even been joking, but the man I was counseling had taken it seriously and made a decision that forever altered his life because he took the advice of fools.

He who walks with wise men will be wise, but the companion of fools will be destroyed.

Proverbs 13:20

He quite possibly could have lived a wonderful life with the love of his life had he chosen godly friends and not listened to worldly counsel.

Change Your Speech

There is one person who speaks to you more than anyone else during the course of the day and that person is you. Like it or not, you give yourself counsel more than anyone else does. The words you speak, whether they are intentional or in jest, contain the power to change your life.

It is possible to speak and create depression, and it is also possible to speak and create hope. The choice of words that come from your mouth rests solely upon you. There is no one else to blame for what you say even though there may be reasons why you speak the way you speak. There are no excuses when it comes to the results.

Think of your words as containers. They can contain faith and hope or they can contain fear and worry. Your words will accomplish what you send them to do.

While we have established that your words proclaim your authority over the enemy, we must never forget that with your words, you prophesy over yourself. One of the most important natural steps you can take in eliminating hopelessness is to prophesy hope over your own life. Quit speaking death into your dream! Quit making statements of defeat! Quit saying, "I can never" and "I will never." Instead start declaring, "I can" and "I will." Quit making excuses! Make the decision to prophesy victory in your life.

Develop a Permanent, Positive Pattern of Living

Throughout recent history, there have been those who have made great achievements in life that have impacted the world. Interestingly, before their great achievements, many of these people were either told their success was impossible or that an insurmountable barrier stood between them and their success. However, neither the words nor the barriers stopped them. They made the decision to believe for the impossible and the impossible became reality.

Albert Einstein was one of the greatest physicists of all time who developed the theory of relativity, which is now one of the pillars of modern physics. In his early years, some of his teachers felt he was not capable because they thought that he had not done well in school by general education standards. However, he excelled in physics and mathematics and he did not give up.

When Jackie Robinson started in baseball, there were no African Americans playing in the major leagues. They were all relegated to a league of their own. He played in the Negro League for a team called the Monarchs which was based in

Kansas City. Even though he was told that playing in the major leagues was impossible for him, he broke through the baseball color barrier when the Brooklyn Dodgers started him at first base in 1947. Jackie Robinson's unquestionable talent and character challenged the segregation which marked American life at that time in history. He became one of the most respected and accomplished players in Major League Baseball history.

Colonel Harland Sanders was told that he should be retiring instead of starting a business when he was 65 years old. He owned one restaurant where he perfected his fried chicken recipe. He saw the potential in franchising restaurants, but had no funds for expansion. So he traveled around the country to different restaurants and cooked his fried chicken right there on the spot for the restaurant owners to eat. If the owners liked the chicken, they entered into a handshake agreement to sell the Colonel's chicken. Legend says that Col. Sanders heard 1,009 "no's" before he heard his first "yes." But that *yes* was the birth of the Kentucky Fried Chicken (KFC) franchise.

Abraham Lincoln was born into a family of poverty. He ran for public office many times and lost many elections by devastating numbers. Yet, he didn't give up his desire to become a leader of the republic. Because he believed in something that looked impossible, he ended up being the 16th President of the United States. His is a true "rags to riches" story.

Had any of these men given up or turned away from the permanent pursuit of their dreams, their stories would not be in this book, and history would not be the same! Dare to continue in the permanent pursuit of your dreams!

Set a Life Pattern

It's always fun to have a day when you have nothing planned—a day of rest, a day of doing nothing, a day of relaxing without responsibility or work. But that should be the exception rather than the pattern for your life. While it does not have to be entirely rigid, your life must have some structure.

Rules and regulations, laws and guidelines throughout life are for the purpose of safety while successfully moving forward. Can you imagine a highway transportation system without any laws regarding speed, turning, changing lanes, or which side of the highway we should drive on? Of course not! The result would be utter chaos, confusion, and certain loss of life.

Likewise, as we travel down the highway of life, there must also be some rules and guidelines. Medically, we know that if you have a pattern of healthy eating and sleeping, your physical life should be longer and more enjoyable. While this can be taken to extremes, extremes usually cause stress. In other words, you can have healthy eating habits and still have a piece of birthday cake. Just don't eat the whole cake every day!

Setting goals and taking on responsibilities should be a part of your life pattern. Likewise, always take time to be thankful. Practice being grateful. Keeping a journal of things you are thankful for can help keep your perspective.

As you plan your lifestyle, there are several things that cannot be ignored that must be included. First and foremost, you must plan for time to worship and praise God, along with time for the study of His Word. Part of this includes finding a church (if you haven't already) that believes the Word of God, that does not preach a politically-correct social gospel, but that believes and practices true Christianity. Without setting aside time for this, nothing else in your plan will work. I call it tithing your time. This should not keep you from being thankful and having an attitude of praise the rest of the time, but your life should reflect the goodness of God.

Have fun! Decide that your life is going to be a life of joy. Do something new. Although you are setting a pattern for life, your life is not meant to be in a rut with mundane, mindless, mechanical duties every day. Look around, add a little spice to your life!

When you do something new, it doesn't necessarily mean that you do it every day. It may only be once, but it can bring freshness and excitement into your life. If you've never been in a boat, go for a boat ride. If you've never been in an airplane, take a flight. If you've never seen snow, go to the mountains. If you've never walked on the beach, go to the ocean. Of course, you can't do these things every day, and you can't do them all at once. But sprinkle these throughout your life, and they will make great memories. They will put a smile on your face, and when a smile is on your face, hopelessness fades.

Don't be selfish and don't be self-centered in life. Look around to see the needs of other people and when possible, lend a helping hand. One of the principles in the Bible is that if you want to receive, you must give (Galatians 6:7). In other words, if you want a harvest in your field, then sow into someone else's field (Luke 6:38). You can't receive without giving.

Develop a Hobby

Everyone should have a hobby. A hobby is something that you do that is enjoyable and outside of your normal daily work.

While your hobby time may not be structured, it should likewise not be ignored.

What are some hobbies? For some people, it's music or sports. For others it's gardening or pets. For some it's gaming, while for others it's building something. There are so many variations of hobbies it is impossible to list all the possibilities, but you must have something in your life you can enjoy and is unique to you.

Let me say this: Watching TV all day is not a hobby. Sleeping is not a hobby. Eating is not a hobby. You should do something that requires mental exercise, has a degree of physical movement, with some type of maintenance.

For example, if gardening is your hobby, weeding and watering are required, but if ignored, your gardening hobby dies. If getting a pet and spending time walking your dog becomes your hobby, of course the dog must be groomed, fed, and cleaned up after. The bottom line in choosing a hobby to relieve hopelessness or despair is that your hobby be something that gets you up off the couch while focusing on something other than the circumstances surrounding you.

Now a word of caution. I have seen people who have started a hobby only to become obsessed with it to the point that everything else in life becomes ignored. Don't do that. Develop a hobby or something that requires maintenance, but balance it in such a way that it does not steal time from your goals or other responsibilities of life.

Be Cautious about Using Medication

I highly recommend that you do not self-diagnose or self-medicate. Do not take drugs or medication on the advice of a friend or relative who is not a medical professional or licensed to prescribe. Many people have made their conditions worse and some have even died because of this. So when it comes to prescribed medication and drugs, be led by the Spirit on what to take. Then only take medication prescribed to you by a licensed professional.

When treating depression or despair, there are many over-the-counter drugs and supplements on the market. I would advise that you do extensive research and use extreme caution rather than making a quick decision to take a drug or a supplement based upon an advertisement or advice from a friend. While there are supplements, vitamins, and drugs that can help, I still strongly advise research and caution before taking them.

Prepare for the Realization of Your Hope

Once you have locked on to God's promise for your situation, next you have to prepare to receive the manifestation of your hope. For example, if you are believing for financial abundance, then you must make plans to use those finances. It can be something as simple as opening an account at the bank to prepare for the harvest.

I know of a guy who had trouble with his legs. He could walk, but his walking was restricted. He was a young man who owned a boat which he could pilot, and he could also drive a car, but otherwise, his physical movement was very limited. He believed so strongly that he was going to be physically healed, that he purchased a gym membership even though at the time he was not capable of walking on a treadmill. But he bought a membership and paid for it in advance because he believed he would need it someday.

If you are incapable of exercise, but you truly believe that the manifestation is on its way, then prepare for it! Get a treadmill for your house. If you truly believe God is going to prosper you, then why wouldn't you open a bank account? Plan ahead and prepare to receive.

Beware of the Imaginary Barrier

I remember years ago when I felt I had a book in my heart that I wanted to write. I was told I would need $5,000 to print the book. I decided when I got $5,000, I would begin to write the book. One time during prayer, I remember God speaking to my heart, saying, "If you had the $5,000 right now, what is the first thing you would do?" My response was, "I would write the manuscript." I heard Him say, "How much would that cost?" My response was, "Nothing." So He said, "Well then, what's stopping you?" What was stopping me was an imaginary barrier.

That was a moment of truth for me. Many times we have excuses for not fulfilling a dream or a destiny, but those excuses are irrelevant. Sometimes the barrier standing between us and the fulfillment of our promise from God is actually an illusion that isn't really there. Yet, because we perceive it to be there, we don't move forward.

Is there an imaginary barrier keeping you from moving forward? Some barriers are real, but many are not. Many imaginary barriers are a result of fearful thinking. Too often a dream or project appears to be so large it looks insurmountable or even impossible to accomplish. But if your dream is from God, then follow the pattern of deliverance that occurred many times in the stories of the Bible. Look at the project honestly and do the possible. Break the project down into smaller, doable sections and do what you can do. When you do what you can do, God will do what you can't do, and your dream will be complete.

For many, the lack of money to complete a project may seem like a barrier, but for others, age may be the barrier, while yet with others it could be gender, race, nationality, or education. History is filled with the names of people who pressed past the barriers and went on to achieve great success.

Maintain a Lifestyle of Hope

How do you maintain a lifestyle of hope? After you obtain hope, you need to know how to maintain it.

Generally, I don't like the concept of diets. It's not that dieting is wrong, but it implies a temporary change in eating habits so the dieter can obtain the desired weight. After the goal has been accomplished, the diet usually ends. Statistics have proven that over time, most dieters regain their weight and then must go on another diet to lose weight again. For many, this cycle continues throughout their lives and dieting becomes the dreaded necessity. For most, but not all, they are counting the days until the diet is over.

The underlying reality is this: if healthy eating habits become a lifestyle, then dieting is not necessary. Once a diet is over and the proper weight is obtained, then a healthy eating lifestyle should negate the need for another crash diet.

In the same way eating healthy can become a lifestyle, living in the realm of faith and hope can become a lifestyle. It's ridiculous to think that we can wait until the enemy hurls his fiery darts before building our shield of faith. Our shield of faith must be continually strengthened to keep quenching the attacks of the enemy. He is relentless. Maintenance must become a lifestyle that never ceases because lowering our faith shields can be deadly. In fact, the enemy is waiting on us to lower them. A lifestyle of faith and hope is not an option, but a necessity.

Don't Give Up

Everything in life increases or decreases; rarely do things stay the same. There are those who feel that their life has never changed, but actually, that is not true. For someone whose today is the same as yesterday and it appears will be the same as their tomorrow, they may claim that nothing changes in their life. Again, that's not true. Although the physical circumstances appear to be the same, hope and desire for the fulfilled dream either increases or decreases as each day passes. Each day the dreams of life either grow or they fade.

Although a Christian has eternal life, physical life on earth is measured. As each day passes, one more day is placed into the past, and there's one less day in the future. To maintain hope, there must be some form of increase. If hope is not daily maintained and confessed, complacency can develop which causes hope to decline. This is why you must never give up your unwavering confession of hope.

> **Let us hold fast the confession of our hope without wavering, for He who promised is faithful.**
>
> Hebrews 10:23 (NASB)

King David Is Your Example

David was the second king of Israel and the father of Solomon. During the reign of Solomon there was great peace in the land, but it was not so under King David. David and his mighty men fought many battles that are recorded in the Bible. But there was a time when David and his mighty men returned to the city of Ziklag only to discover that their city had been burned to the ground. The Amalekites, who had invaded the city, took all the women and the remaining population as prisoners and fled. When David and his men returned to the city, seeing it was burned and their wives, sons, and daughters were led away captive, they dropped to the ground, lifted their voices, and cried until they had no more power to cry.

King David had two wives, Ahinoam and Abigail, who had also been taken away. Of course, David was distressed, but his mighty men were so grieved for their sons and daughters they considered killing David.

How much worse could things be? David's wives were taken, along with the wives and children of all his soldiers. His soldiers, who were battle trained, were talking of killing their leader. What could David do? What were his options when it appeared that he had no options? He did the thing that every person feeling hopeless should do. He turned to God and encouraged himself in the greatness of God (1 Samuel 30:1-6.)

> **Now David was greatly distressed, for the people spoke of stoning him, because the soul of all the people was grieved, every man for his sons and his daughters. But David strengthened himself in the Lord his God.**
>
> **1 Samuel 30:6**

The end result was this: the impossible became possible and the possible became victory. Everything the enemy had stolen was recovered (1 Samuel 30:17-20). This story about David is your template for recovery and restoration. God is no respecter of persons (Acts 10:34 KJV). If He did it for David, He'll do it for you!

> For whatever things were written before were written for our learning, that we through the patience and comfort of the Scriptures might have hope.
>
> Romans 15:4

Your Testimony

> But sanctify the Lord God in your hearts, and always be ready to give a defense to everyone who asks you a reason for the hope that is in you, with meekness and fear.
>
> 1 Peter 3:15

In this book, several examples have been given of how people have overcome impossible odds and succeeded in defeating depression and words of discouragement to achieve the goal God put in their heart.

But before we close this book, I would like to give one more example. This example is *you!* I want you to pause right now to imagine seeing yourself as God created you to be. See your life as a testimony of victory that others can see and be inspired. See yourself as an example of deliverance. See yourself walking in the fullness of life that God has promised you. See yourself free from depression. See yourself full of hope.

With biblical hope established in your heart, hopelessness has become a memory. With the disappointments of life behind you and knowing that the promises of God are true, you are now able to step forward into the peace, rest, and joy that await you. Your best days are yet to come!

Bibliography

Blue Letter Bible. "Dictionary and Word Search for *qavah (Strong's 6960)*." Blue Letter Bible. 1996-2017. [Online]. http://www.blbclassic.org/lang/lexicon/Lexicon.cfm?Strongs=H6960&t=KJV [2017 July].

Blue Letter Bible. "Dictionary and Word Search for *tikvah (Strong's 8615)*." Blue Letter Bible. 1996-2017. [Online]. http://www.blbclassic.org/lang/lexicon/lexicon.cfm?Strongs=H8615&t=KJV [2017 July].

Gallagher, K. (2013). "What is Biblical Hope?" [Online]. https://graceintorah.net/2013/10/26/tikvah-hope. [2017 July].

Ollison, Larry. *The Power of Grace*. Tulsa: Harrison House Publishers, 2013.

Other books by Dr. Larry Ollison
available through Harrison House Publishers

Life is in the Blood
Discover the Power of the Blood of Jesus
ISBN# 9780965320238

The Practical Handbook for Christian Living
*The Believer's Guide to Growing in
Christ and Living with Purpose*
ISBN# 9781606833544

The Power of Grace
*How You Can Access God's Unlimited
Power to Accomplish the Impossible*
ISBN# 9781606836675

Breaking the Cycle of Offense
*Living Free from Offense Is One of the Most
Important Subjects that a Christian Can Master*
ISBN# 9781930027961

The Paradise of God
*Discover the Biblical Truth about Heaven
and Unlock the Mystery of Life after Death*
ISBN# 9781606838679

Unlocking the Mysteries of the Holy Spirit
*God's Desire Is for His Believers to Know
and Understand the Deep Things of the Spirit*
ISBN# 9781680310535

A Place Called Heaven
Your Journey Home
ISBN# 9781680314977

Hidden Mysteries and the Bible
*Secrets Revealed: Aliens/UFOs, Giants, Time Travel,
Multiverse, AI & Other Unexplained Phenomena*
ISBN# 9781667502984

PRAYER OF SALVATION

God loves you—no matter who you are, no matter what your past. God loves you so much that He gave His one and only begotten Son for you. The Bible tells us that "...whoever believes in him shall not perish but have eternal life" (John 3:16 NIV). Jesus laid down His life and rose again so that we could spend eternity with Him and experience His absolute best on earth. If you would like to receive Jesus into your life, say the following prayer out loud and mean it in your heart.

Heavenly Father, I come to you admitting that I am a sinner. Right now, I choose to turn away from sin, and I ask you to cleanse me of all unrighteousness. I believe that Your son, Jesus, died on the cross to take away my sins. I also believe that He rose again from the dead so that I might be forgiven of my sins and made righteous through faith in Him. I call upon the name of Jesus Christ to be the Savior and Lord of my life. Jesus, I choose to follow You and ask that You fill me with the power of the Holy Spirit. I declare that right now I am a child of God. I am free from sin and full of the righteousness of God. I am saved in Jesus' name. Amen.

If you prayed this prayer to receive Jesus Christ as your Savior for the first time, please write to us to receive a free book!

www.harrisonhouse.com
Harrison House Publishers
P.O. Box 310
Shippensburg, PA 17257

The Harrison House Vision

Proclaiming the truth and the power

Of the Gospel of Jesus Christ

With excellence;

Challenging Christians to

Live victoriously,

Grow spiritually,

Know God intimately.

Fast. Easy.
Convenient.

For the latest Harrison House product information and author news, look no further than your computer. All the details on our powerful, life-changing products are just a click away. New releases, e-mail subscriptions, testimonies, monthly specials — find it all in one place. Visit **harrison**house.com today!

harrisonhouse.com